THE
ONLY
BLACK
MAN
IN THE
ROOM

Jamar J. Hébert

J.HÉBERT
COMPANIES

A J. Hébert Companies Publication

The Only Black Man in the Room
Published by a division of J. Hébert Companies, LLC.
Newberry, FL, USA www.jamarhebert.com

Contributing Editors: Daron Christopher, Thomas Hauck, and LaToia Burkley, CPDC, ACC.

Featured Contributing Editor: Robert L. Stevenson, Jr., PhD. (Historical Perspective)

Cover Design: Aaron Daye for Gorilla Ink

Author Photos Credit: James Hardy Photography and Smiling Good Photography

For information about special discounts available for bulk purchases, sales promotions, fund-raising and educational needs, contact J. Hébert Companies, LLC. Sales at info@jamarhebert.com or call 225-937-6236.

Library of Congress Cataloging-In-Publication Data

Hébert, Jamar, 1979-

The Only Black Man in the Room

ISBN Paperback: 978-0-9997565-2-2

ISBN Hardback: 978-0-9997565-5-3

ISBN Digital: 978-0-9997565-1-5

Library of Congress Control Number: 2022910823

PRINTED IN THE UNITED STATES OF AMERICA

Dedication

For the two young men in our family, Jarius and Maddox,
and the women who make our lives so special:
Our daughters Peyton and Morgan.

Contents

Foreword

Thomas W. Dortch, Jr.

Since our first chapter was founded in New York City in 1963, our inspiring motto, "What They See Is What They'll Be," has captured the spirit of the 100 Black Men of America.

Our origins began with a small group of visionary businessmen and industry leaders, among them such stalwarts as Jackie Robinson and future New York City Mayor David Dinkins.

In the decades since, there have been times when it's been easy to despair over a lack of progress in racial relations. Honest conversations around our national legacy of racial strife remains a "third rail," with many of our fellow citizens still unable or unwilling to confront "our original sin"—the stain that slavery, segregation, and mass incarceration have left on our national character and psyche.

Yet it's also impossible to deny the enormous strides we have made since 1963. For example, at that time, African-American police officers in our nation's largest city were forbidden from arresting a White citizen without a White police officer present.

Think about that. They were forbidden by one of the very same policies they had taken an oath to uphold and for which they risked their lives each day to maintain.

When one Black officer broke the law and arrested a White citizen—in short, when he did his job—an uproar broke out.

Men like Jackie Robinson, David Dinkins, Dr. William Hayling, Andrew Hatcher, Edison Wingate, and others had seen enough. With a system so clearly tilted against young men of color, there was a clear need for an organization that would harness the collective power of African-American men and provide a platform for mentoring and championing the next generation.

They named it 100 Black Men, and the organization rapidly grew far broader in scope. In 1986 it was formally enshrined as a national organization, and today boasts chapters in more than 103 cities across the nation and other countries.

Our continued success today as an organization is thanks to the dedication, passion, and civic spirit of the local Black male community leaders who freely give of their time, talent, and treasures to give back to our young men and women.

Jamar Hébert is the embodiment of that spirit of service. A family man with a successful career in business and telecommunications, Jamar has no shortage of demands on his time. Yet like so many civic leaders I have met across the country, he is not one to pull up the ladder behind him when he succeeds. He is not one for self-glorification or resting on his laurels. On the contrary, he continues to extend that ladder of possibility to others so that they can follow in his footsteps.

Jamar knows from experience what men like Jackie Robinson and David Dinkins experienced throughout their careers, and what it's like to be the only Black man in the room. His story is one of pride, empathy, and resolve.

Under his leadership, 100 Black Men of Greater Florida, Gainesville gives hope, guidance, opportunity, and self-respect to a growing network of young men who will go on to be leaders in our public life, business community, military, arts, and any other endeavor they set their minds to accomplishing.

Throughout my own career, I learned firsthand that being the first Black man in any room is a point of pride, whether the room is the Oval Office, the operating room, or city hall. But what truly matters, beyond being first, is what you do to open pathways of opportunity for others. Any success I have experienced for myself has always paled in comparison to the feeling of pride I have gained from service, mentoring, and counsel to others.

Too many of our young people still lack someone actively present in their lives who can present a model for a path through a world that is still too often tilted against African-Americans. The COVID-19 pandemic has only exacerbated this challenge by exposing the inequities in our society and driving so many of our young people apart into isolation in the name of public safety, just when they need community and strong role models more than ever.

In telling his story, Jamar has created a natural extension of his work mentoring and serving his community. He dives deep in creating a priceless gift for those young men. Indeed, "What they see is what they'll be."

And in his story, I come away with renewed pride in how far we have come as a people – through self-determination, hard work, and love for one another.

Sincerely,

Thomas W. Dortch, Jr.
National Chairman – 100 Black Men of America

Preface

This book was on my mind long before the events of 2020 came along and turned everything that our country knew upside down.

I suddenly found myself, like most people, spending much more time at home. I hadn't spent three straight weeks in my home in maybe 20 years. Suddenly, we all had a strange new environment to navigate, as the threat of the COVID-19 pandemic kept more of us indoors.

Yet even as I recognized my good fortune in having a safe home to shelter in—one filled with loved ones, good food, and entertainment to give my weary mind a distraction from the news of the day—I recognized that outside, events marched on. Even as we were urged to socially and physically distance ourselves from one another, it became increasingly clear to many Black people that this was not the time to turn our back on each other or our communities.

While the virus was nominally colorblind, our institutions were not. The virus ripped through communities of color—Black, Latinx, and Indigenous American—with a disproportionate ferocity that could only be a surprise to someone who hadn't been paying attention. People of color make up an outsized percentage of the essential workers who never had the opportunity to telework or shelter in place. They were needed to keep the country moving forward each day by processing food, working in hospitals and rest homes, serving as dental assistants, being home health aides, and driving the buses that got all the other essential workers home each evening.

I think about my baby sister Lacie, a nurse practitioner in Louisiana who, like so many health professionals across the country, got up each day and went to work on the front lines combatting the virus. Even when sent out to what could feel like the public health equivalent of a warzone without the necessary levels of personal protective equipment, despite the risks to themselves, she and thousands of others showed up each day as consummate professionals.

Many paid the ultimate price for their heroism. People whom we often deem to be worth no more than minimum wage showed how truly indispensable they were to keeping our society moving forward each day.

The toll quickly became clear. By June 2020, 11 percent of Black people personally knew someone who had died from COVID-19, compared to only 4 percent of White Americans—a grim accounting of the underlying chronic health conditions rampant in many communities of color, from diabetes to hypertension. As of May 2020, researchers found that disproportionately Black counties made up more than half of coronavirus cases, and 60 percent of deaths.

Sadly, the response by the federal government, and specifically the White House, seemed like something out of the era of Jim Crow. As Adam Serwer wrote his article for *The Atlantic* entitled "The Coronavirus Was an Emergency Until Trump Found Out Who Was Dying," the Trump administration, "in carrying out an explicitly discriminatory agenda that valorizes cruelty, war crimes, and the entrenchment of white political power," represented "a revitalized commitment to the racial contract," which was the unspoken rule that the invisible social contract between White and Black people in America had been written to favor the White establishment.

This was only the latest clear example of the ways that Black and White Americans often find themselves living in vastly different universes. Many of our fellow citizens have seldom ever fully inhabited the universe in which young Black men without a high school diploma are more likely to be found in a prison cell than the workplace, and in which the net worth of the average household headed by a White person is nearly ten times than that of a household headed by a Black person.

It's a world in which only 17 percent of Black men hold a bachelor's degree, compared to 30 percent of all men. In 2017, the number of Black college students was estimated to be 3.3 million—a *decrease* from 3.6 million just seven years earlier. That's a change in the wrong direction.

The year 2020 was one of reckoning. Perhaps it was the disproportionate toll the pandemic was taking, or the sheer frustration that followed months of lockdown. Perhaps it was the inevitable explosion after years of each police shooting adding more kindling to the growing fire. Maybe it was the horrific cell phone footage that captured each moment in brutal detail of Minneapolis Police Officer Derek Chauvin carrying out the cold-blooded murder of George Floyd, and the fact that Chauvin knew he was acting with impunity.

Think of all the police actions we *didn't* see on cell phone videos. Think of all the names we never heard.

We've seen too many young Black men and women become public figures not because they had the opportunity to fulfill their full talents, but because they were struck down senselessly by those whom our society has charged with protecting them.

Wherever it came from, the murder of George Floyd over Memorial Day weekend sparked something new in American life. This time, it truly did feel different.

The protests that erupted in the months following may well become the largest mass protests in contemporary American life. The images look vastly different when we compare them to the iconic images of marches across places like Selma and Montgomery in the late 1960s. Today's protesters dress more informally, for one thing. They are savvier about generating attention in today's social-media saturated culture.

But most crucially, they are joined by more of their White neighbors than ever before. Today's Black Lives Matter movement has emerged as a truly multi-ethnic coalition, in which more White citizens have boldly decided to actively critique and work to dismantle a system they cannot deny has benefitted them.

And while there are some—depending on where they get their news and their information—who have seen images of social unrest and have embraced the fear of the left-wing bogeyman known as "Antifa," what I have felt is *hope*. I see a country finally owning up to the legacy of our country's original sins, and the promise of a new generation that won't accept a society that is separate and unequal.

Many White people have joined as allies, but many more remain skeptical. Particularly outside of young and highly educated urban communities, distrust and skepticism remain widespread over the notion that the United States still has work to do in order to dismantle a racist power structure.

Social media is a good start for getting the conversation going, but, as much as we can in a pandemic, we have to take the action offline. We have to put the work in. If we aren't doing the work ourselves, we can't look for it from our elected officials, the media, or corporate America.

That brings us to this book. There are many stories and perspectives available on the subject of race in America. Mine represents just one— my own perspective on what it's like to live as a man in a business and professional world that has been, intentionally or not, built for people who don't look like me.

I'm not interested in vilifying, demonizing, or scapegoating. On the contrary, I have been inspired by the recent movement to find a way to play a constructive dialogue in driving greater understanding and discussion among Black and White Americans. My hope is that regardless of your background or where you come from, these pages will challenge you, inspire you, and help you to see the world in a different way.

Many Black folks are well accustomed to feeling alienated in America, and certainly don't need my words to understand what it's like. My hope for my Black brothers and sisters is that I can provide concrete, actionable steps on what they can do to ensure their success and happiness when they find themselves, as I so often have, The Only Black Man in the Room.

Introduction

If you are a Black man, or the parent or spouse of one, and you're seeking to build a better life for yourself according to the promise of the American Dream, this book is for you.

If you are a White person, and you're interested in gaining a better understanding of the unique perspectives held by Black men as they make their way through a world that presents them with conflicting messages, this book is for you.

I say "conflicting messages" because *on paper*, the United States of America is a pretty great place to live. We've got democracy, capitalism, personal freedom, equal opportunity, the possibility of abundant wealth—all the good things anyone could hope for.

But *in reality*, it's not so simple. Our system is far from perfect. We face massive income inequality, political division, discrimination, and other problems. And there is one challenge faced uniquely by most Black people in America: Unlike any other racial or ethnic group, for the first 246 years of the Black experience in North America, the vast majority of Black people were held in bondage, as enslaved people. They were legally *non-human*. That's a heavy thought, isn't it? Emancipation came in 1865, but that didn't settle the issue; for the next century and beyond, the White power structure endeavored to limit and stifle Black participation in the American Dream. This effort was often brutal and violent, and Black people who attempted to claim their rightful place could be killed with impunity.

But you know all of that. And you also know that despite the pious assertions by some that we are living in a "post-racial" society, serious inequity persists. Racist violence against innocent Black citizens is all too common. Workplace inequality still exists. It's still very likely that if you're a Black man and you're working at a company or in public service, you'll find yourself to be literally the Only Black Man in the Room.

This book is a modest attempt to help today's Black man navigate this uncertain world, to change what he can, and survive what he can't.

I have split the book into five sections.

Chapter 1 is my story.

Chapter 2 is specifically geared to White people, but of course, anyone is welcome to read it.

Chapter 3 is aimed at Black men—but again, if you're not a member of that group, I hope you'll check it out.

Chapter 4 presents my carefully selected group of OBMIR Success Stories from past and present.

Chapter 5 features my practical, down-to-earth Five Tips to Own the Room.

My intent is not to segregate the readership or to speak out of two sides of my mouth. My goal is to underscore how we continue, decades after landmark steps like Brown v. Board of Education, to live in completely separate universes, even when occupying the same physical space at our offices, schools, places of worship, and communities.

You, dear reader, are invited to read all sections! My hope is that I'll be able to shed some light for the White reader on what it's like to operate primarily in rooms filled with people who don't look like you, who often approach the world with a completely different cultural context.

As I mentioned, Chapter 2 presents a viewpoint that many may think is unusual. It's written specifically to reach out to my White brothers and sisters on how it feels to be the only Black man in "the room" – the room being any professional setting, be it a medical office, corporate board room, church, all the way to the Oval Office in the White House.

In recent years, an increasing number of empathetic White Americans have sought a greater understanding of what it's like to walk in the shoes of their Black neighbors. While there are no definitive tracts on the Black experience in America—the subject is too vast for any one book—I hope to make a modest contribution through these reflections.

The most well-meaning of our White brothers and sisters may not fully understand how systemic racism, the long legacy of discrimination over centuries in America, and cultural roadblocks have resulted in countless Black people finding themselves being the only Black person at the table in their workplace. As Sharon Chuter, CEO, founder, and creative director of Uoma Beauty said, "My entire corporate career, I was always the only Black person at the organization. There was never a meeting I went to, even globally, where there was another Black person in the room. Never. These are the things that really need to change."

In addition to carrying the burden of stereotypes and preconceptions, the Black person is often given the absurd task of being asked to *represent their entire race*. As one Black person is judged, so is every Black person, everywhere.

If you're a White person, take a moment to ponder that ridiculous thought.

Times are changing, and we have seen extraordinary progress over decades. I would never dispute our advancements, but we have a long way to go. Far too many Black people are still made to feel "less than." Too many are treated differently, with their identities disrespected. This is often done behind closed doors, but sometimes in the bright light of day.

The purpose of this book is to provide perspective from my own experience and the experiences of others, past and present, along with actionable tips, strategies, and thoughts on how to successfully navigate this environment. The goal is to not simply *survive*, but *thrive*.

Ready? Let's get started!

1

CHAPTER 1
My Story

My story begins in the city of my birth, Baton Rouge, Louisiana. As Drake Aubrey Graham once put it, "I'm hardly home, but always reppin'!" I wasn't exactly an Eagle Scout, but I did gravitate early on to opportunities in volunteerism and service.

I came of age during a time just a generation removed from the heroics of the height of the Civil Rights Movement and the watershed marches that led to landmark legislation like the Voting Rights Act of 1964 and the Fair Housing Act of 1965.

For my mother, Wanda, these stories were not sepia-toned pages in a history book; they were her reality. She attended the Catholic High School of Pointe Coupee, a Catholic Interparochial school in New Roads, Louisiana. Founded in 1904 by the Sisters of St. Joseph who were commissioned to bring Catholic education to Pointe Coupee Parish, at the time the student body was nearly all White, with Wanda being one of the few exceptions.

My mother Wanda graduated from Catholic High of Pointe Coupee, a Catholic Interparochial school in New Roads, Louisiana.

This was at the very height of the Civil Rights movement. She was part of just the second class to integrate the school, so she stuck out plenty to her peers. There were many times she was the only girl in the room, enduring taunting and spitting just for the crime of trying to get an education. Among other epithets, she was called a "locust"—coming from people who took the Book of Exodus seriously, this was a nasty insult.

As bad as today's climate can be, it's undeniable that the kind of overt everyday hate my mother and her few Black classmates endured would be grounds for censure today. One of her history teachers, who pulled double duty as the football coach, would tell his class with its one Black player, "As much as I like Eugene, if we had to have a race war, I would let him go."

Once, my mother's home economics teacher issued a class assignment in which the students had to purchase sewing materials to make whatever they wanted. My mother decided to purchase some bright green, red, and yellow fabric to make a scarf. Her home economics teacher responded with, "That's not the colors you want. Do you know what you would look like in that?"

She persisted and made it through that toxic environment. She did all that not just for herself, but because she knew, on some level, she was paving the way for those who would come after her. That's the unique burden that so many Black folks face; it's not simply enough to strive for themselves, but they need to always ensure they remain "a credit to the race," thereby smoothing the way for those who follow.

The same was true for my aunt Gloria, a member of the first class to integrate Pointe Coupee during her 6th grade year in 1971-1972. She persisted and became the only Black cheerleader, and then the first Black homecoming queen contestant for the Class of 1978.

1978
Catholic High of Pointe Coupee Cheerleaders

My aunt Gloria was the first Black cheerleader at her high school. She went on to be the first Black student to run for homecoming queen and ultimately served on the court.

Some considered her to be the best cheerleader the school had ever seen, with a unique voice that was also up to the challenge of imitating iconic singers like Tina Turner and Gladys Knight. But despite her obvious talent, it took three years of tryouts for the cheerleading squad before she finally made the team in her junior year.

Every little bit of progress seemed to come as "one step forward, one step back." Maybe younger generations are a little bit more inclined to the idea of change. Gloria's White peers voted for her. A White boy even dated her, and used to come visit the family throughout the early '70s. But when he told his parents that he was in love with my aunt, they were horrified, and that was the end of that.

As for my father, Lionel Hébert, he grew up in the small town of Oscar, Louisiana. His childhood played out against the vistas of a plantation called Cherie Quarters.

Growing up in Oscar, Lionel understood pretty quickly that he was poor. He had to wash his face with cold water from a faucet and take baths in a tub outside. The old folks would kill hogs and use grease to wash their faces. The only time my father and his siblings felt embarrassed was when friends came to visit. It was then impossible to hide the poverty his family was experiencing.

Hébert family portrait archives – Oscar, Louisiana at Cherie Quarters - 1960s.

His parents taught him how to conduct himself around White people, and that there were certain things he should and should not do. This is a common experience for Black kids: learning the proper rules and etiquette for the delicate work of navigating a White world. He learned to always bow his head, display deference to white adults, and to say, "Yes, ma'am; no, ma'am; yes, sir; no sir." He was taught how to reassure White people that he understood his proper role in the social and economic hierarchy.

His mother – who I knew as Maw Maw Carrie - always worked to feed her family, but even as a little kid, my father understood that in regard to the amount of money his mom was being paid, she was routinely cheated.

It wasn't until the age of fifteen, when Lionel entered the workforce, that he realized how prejudiced White people could be in his community. His first job was working at Triple Large Restaurant on the weekends, earning $7 a day. This was considered a lot of money back then. Because he worked in the kitchen, where the White customers couldn't see him, he didn't face much racism on the job. He was impressed by the Black workers who knew how to operate the cash register. The White folks had grudging respect for them—they had to be smarter than the average Black person if they were doing all that math!

The old folks would tell Lionel that he needed to go to school and get an education. Against stacked odds, that seemed like the only hope for success.

It wasn't long before Lionel's natural restlessness kicked in and he yearned for more. His goal in life was to get away from working in the kitchen and from Oscar, so at the tender age of sixteen he left Louisiana to attend the Gary Job Corps Center in San Marcos, Texas. (Founded by Sargent Shriver in 1964, it's still there today, offering the opportunity for young people of all races to improve the quality of their lives through career technical and academic training.)

His mind was made up: the path out of poverty was to learn a trade. He earned a certificate of completion as well as his GED; he later described it as "the best move he had ever made." He ultimately achieved his goal of becoming an entrepreneur as a restaurant owner. My father wanted his own business because, as he would often tell me, he didn't believe in working for other people when he could work for himself.

"Sit down, come up with a plan, and just do it," he said. Years later, I thought that sounded like a pretty good title for a book!

I can still vividly remember my greatest honor of my own childhood. It was not an accolade in sports or even the classroom. (And it definitely didn't come in my first job as a valet parking attendant!) It came when I received the Brotherhood Sisterhood Award from the NCCJ National Coalition of Christians and Jews. Since 1963, the Brotherhood Sisterhood

Awards have recognized individuals in the community who have worked toward the elimination of bias, bigotry and racism across ethnic, gender and religious lines. I earned it for "commitment to the advancement of justice, amity, and peace." Those were lofty words for my modest efforts, and I've striven to live up to them ever since. Wherever I have lived and no matter how busy I've been, I've tried to always carve out time to give back to my community. Not because I'm a saint—far from it. I've actually found that it can feel selfish at times, because being involved in community work makes me feel better, has helped me build a network of contacts and wonderful friends, and leaves me with a smile on my face as the worries of my own day-to-day preoccupations fade from my thoughts. My advice to anyone looking for a pick-me-up is to go help someone else. It can work wonders for you, and leave someone else better off in the process.

It's funny, looking back later when you connect the dots and reflect on how you arrived at the interests and passions that drive you as an adult. I knew racism was a factor in the world growing up; if you're Black in America, that's unavoidable. But I grew up in comparatively tranquil times. Racial tensions would flare up, but some degree of racism just seemed to be the way of the world. Maybe we just had to accept it.

My entire perspective changed when I accepted an invitation to go see a movie, not knowing anything about it or even the title.

It turned out to be *Rosewood*, directed by the late, great John Singleton. Talk about the only Black man in the room! In 1989, Singleton was the first Black person ever nominated for Best Director at the Academy Awards. (And he did it at the ripe old age of 24 for the remarkable *Boyz N Da Hood*—a clear demonstration that the old don't have any monopoly on wisdom.)

If you don't know *Rosewood*, it tells the story of a Florida town that was all but destroyed in the name of racism and hate. I was a bit embarrassed about how much of the history of my community I didn't know. I was captivated and immediately begged my mother to purchase a copy of the book. I stayed up late into the night reading about the history of this town and the massacre of its Black citizens.

Life can turn out funny. It was almost two decades later that I would become a Floridian myself, building a home for my family in the Gainesville area that's less than 45 minutes away from Rosewood—a fact I was unaware of until a fellow neighbor educated me on just how close we were living to this grim bit of American history.

In the tranquility of my yard in the evening, spending time with our wonderful children, it's hard to believe that such hatred could have played out just down the road from us.

But that's the tragic story of America and the paradox of a country that offers incredible opportunities for anyone willing to work hard, but also demands Black people work twice as hard as White people for the same reward. It's the paradox of a nation where Black people in certain fields have been given incredible opportunities to maximize their potential, while so many others find themselves languishing far below what they are capable of, unable to emerge from under a heap of obstacles and barriers that White people don't seem to face.

I'm acutely aware that for many people, especially young boys and young men of color, minor mistakes can be enough for disqualification from playing the game entirely. Dabbling in recreational drugs like marijuana can be a rite of passage or time of experimentation for many young, White Americans; the same offense can more often than not land a young Black man in prison for years, even decades. All you can say is, "There but for the grace of God go I."

The combined legacy of "The Just Say No" movement of the 1980s and the multi-decade War on Drugs waged in America has been soaring arrest and incarceration disparities for communities of color. In fact, nearly 80 percent of those in federal prison and nearly 60 percent in state prisons for drug offenses are either Black or Latino. Just imagine the landmines that young Black men must walk in resisting ordinary temptations and rites of passage; what can be an "experiment" for a young White student can more often than not be a life-ruining fork in the road for a young person of color.

The truth is that my hard work doesn't make me exceptional; it has been a serendipitous blend of luck and grace that has enabled me to thrive and live a productive, fulfilled life.

How many of us fall into what W.E.B. DuBois called "the talented tenth," a term that designated a leadership class of Black people in the early 20th century?

For many young people, the primary focus lays more heavily on simply surviving into adulthood in a world that seldom awards second chances.

My Brother, Christopher

My brother, Christopher, understands what it was like growing up in our environment. (He could also be a real pain sometimes, but that's just how brothers are!) He went on to a remarkable career in the legal profession in our native state, rising to serve under the Louisiana Attorney General and going on to overseeing the state's gaming division.

But none of it was a foregone conclusion when we were growing up. Christopher rarely has wanted to dwell on it, but he seemed to face situation after situation in which he was called into question in ways that just simply don't tend to happen to White folks.

He did well in school academically from early on and went on to a virtually all-White Catholic school. He had offers for basketball scholarships from top high schools in our hometown of Baton Rouge, but Catholic High stood out for its reputation for great academics. Our mother insisted that he attend on an academic scholarship, not one for athletics.

My brother wasn't especially excited about the prospect of attending an all-boys school, but he understood that he was being presented with an opportunity at a great education.

It was an adjustment, however. It was his first experience in an academic environment that wasn't made up of majority Black students.

After early years of classrooms that reflected the diversity of our city and region, stepping foot into that environment was something of a culture shock. My brother could count on just two hands the number of Black students in the entire school, from grades 9 to 12, including only three in his freshman class.

The problem with environments lacking in any kind of diversity is that they have a way of establishing cultural mores without ever considering how they could impact different types of people.

Like the time my brother was suspended on account of his haircut; it was deemed "not acceptable" because of how *short* it was cut *on the sides*. (In most schools, having hair that's too *long* on the sides is the problem. Go figure.) He was a freshman, and had been participating in the school talent show. When he was done performing, in the midst of audience members coming up to congratulate him, a teacher appeared and informed him that he would be disciplined "until the hair grows back on his sides."

By the way, as a 48-year-old professional, my brother maintains the same haircut today.

This was not an isolated incident. My brother didn't and does not today define himself by how others see him. He does not consider himself a victim. Yet it is impossible to ignore all the petty slights and aggressions that he endured, including teammates calling him the "n" word to his face.

It was a tough environment to navigate, let alone thrive. My brother found his grades slipping and tells me that to this day he has a negative taste in his mouth about that school. I know that he has spoken with kids who have attended more recently and found them seeming to face so many of the same challenges—think of common hairstyles like dreadlocks and braids landing kids in suspension. It can be depressing to reflect on how we continue to fight so many of the same battles after so long.

These slights followed him to college, where a teacher simply couldn't believe that he had the writing talent to turn in a stellar paper. It didn't matter that his favorite subject was English; his professor simply couldn't fathom that his work would be up to that quality. The teacher accused him of buying his paper.

The dean assured him he would look into the charge and have it stricken from his record. That didn't happen. It surfaced some seven years later when he was taking the bar exam. It's easy to see how a few thoughtless actions on the part of others can dramatically throw someone off the course of pursuing their dreams, at no fault of their own.

Like the time Christopher went into K-Mart on a rare cold day in Louisiana. He wore a heavy trench coat that day to stay warm—that's how cold it was! We just aren't used to plummeting temperatures in Louisiana. He had picked up some earmuffs in the store and had considered buying them, but then he put them back on the shelf. He left the store. When he got to his car in the parking lot, store security approached him. (He could hear our mother's voice say, "Keep cool and keep your hands visible!") They told him to get out of the car. ("Always comply, no matter how unfair the command!") He was searched thoroughly, and they found no contraband. They let him go. This was before my brother began his legal career—he likely didn't even know that he was being searched illegally. (Not that it would have made any difference if he had known.)

It may not sound like much to someone who hasn't experienced it. But an experience like this, which can be imposed on a person of color at any time while carrying out the most mundane of activities, can have a traumatic effect over time.

My brother and I are of common mind about these incidents. We are not defined by them. We don't sit around brooding about them incessantly. But it's never too far from our minds, even if we would prefer otherwise, to consider that a certain segment of society will always look at us with suspicion, no matter what uniform of respectability we may wear. A business suit has a way of putting people at ease, but only for so long. We know we are only one hoodie away from our colleagues tensing up again. It seems like we can strive for excellence, and still be largely considered in the context of our skin pigment.

If there is a silver lining to stories like my brother's, it is that they prepared him to endure and to withstand anything that life threw at him. He has been ready to navigate the terrain as often the only Black person at the conference and speaking circuit in his industry. He's been prepared for the pettiness we see so often today; like when a colleague failed to recognize him without his standard uniform of a suit and tie and crossed the street to avoid him, all because his casual jeans and T-shirt sent a message that he was someone to be feared.

The Drive to Succeed

My family instilled in me a drive to succeed. They laid out a canvas to dream big and to not lower my sights because of challenges I would face along the way.

I was lucky. I grew up in an environment in which everyone in my life pushed me to have high expectations of myself. I had my grandfather, my mother, and my brother to emulate in their examples of not settling for anything less than their very best.

It was because of their examples that my brother and I learned to dream big; and my brother went to serve as an assistant attorney general for the State of Louisiana.

But my parents were also clear-eyed about the very real obstacles that young Black men face. I think they sought for as long as possible to shield me from a full understanding of the odds stacked against me from a statistical perspective.

Paw-Paw

My grandfather stood as one of the towering role models of my early life, and through to this day. His name was Lawrence Louis, Jr. I knew him only as Paw-Paw.

He was born in 1915—not an easy time for Black men, who were especially targeted by violently racist groups such as the Klan as well as the implicitly racist economic and political establishment.

But despite the circumstances he was born into, he did not allow his station in life to deter him from achieving the American dream. My grandfather achieved all of his dreams—home ownership, a proud family life, and a distinguished military service career. And he did it all without a high school diploma or college degree. Those doors were largely shut to him because of the prejudices of the time.

There were many things I didn't know about him, and learned only later in life. It was at Paw-Paw's funeral that I heard this story from my uncle during his eulogy.

My grandfather had returned from serving in World War II. He had put his body on the line and helped to liberate a continent and preserve a democratic way of life for a world that was in real danger of being overrun by a mad man.

And how was he greeted when he returned to the States?

While heading back home from New Jersey to Louisiana, the bus made a stop in Mississippi. The Black men aboard weren't exactly greeted by the locals with respect for their military service; to the contrary, they were told, "Y'all niggers, don't let the sun go down on you." That meant that after dark, you'd better not be seen in any public place.

It was not exactly the stuff of a ticker tape parade. Paw-Paw and his fellow service members, having served in segregated units, were even met at the train station by the local police upon their arrival home. Law enforcement made it known to them that it was in their best interest to get home before dawn.

They had gone off and fought for the idea of a free society and free people, only to find themselves viewed as second-class citizens, even while wearing the uniform.

Change came slowly, at least in terms of the law. On July 26, 1948, President Harry S. Truman signed Executive Order 9981, thereby taking the (sadly) courageous step of desegregating the armed forces, a step that would have been unfathomable at the height of conscription during the war effort.

My grandfather went on to a long, dignified, professional life working in a local plant. That was a story he never told me. He came up in a time when everyday petty mistreatment was to be expected. He found his stature in transcending those ugly moments, keeping his head down, and focusing on what he could control—giving back to his community and supporting his family.

In his heart, he understood that his personal struggles could not be separated from the struggles of the Black community at large. In the 1960s, he joined a boycott of a local racist grocery store. Immediately after getting off from work, he would walk the picket line until nine o'clock at night.

I have to believe that were he with us today, he would recognize that the time for "turning the other cheek" has long passed. I think he would be in the streets with the kids.

Every person and every free society have their breaking point.

Looking Back

I've worked hard to achieve a successful career in the world of business, primarily focusing on telecommunications. I remember the hard, long nights it took to advance and the sacrifices I made to live out a career I'm passionate about. I'm grateful to have been given opportunities to work hard at work that was worth doing in this country, but I'm also acutely aware that my experience is also one of good fortune. We all stand on the shoulders of others, and my own good fortunate—a success story that some cynical people might point to as proof that systemic racism is not with us—doesn't negate the reality that for far too many people with whom I grew up in Louisiana, their experience has been that of moving through life with a boot forever on their neck.

I saw it in the years before COVID-19 struck, when I would go home for the Fourth of July. This is a holiday that many Black people, even the most devout patriots, view with mixed feelings. It's the feeling of seeing someone you care about fall short of what you know they are capable of. That is how so many of us have felt, especially in recent years when numbing episodes of police brutality have reminded us of how far we still have to go in the post-Obama era.

Just as we can't extrapolate the meteoric success of a few brilliant individuals like President Obama to mean that we no longer have an opportunity gap, I must continue to remind myself that my own advancement can't replace the advancement of our people. I've been honored to work with a wide range of organizations doing remarkable work in my community, in time making me feel like a true Floridian. These include the Boys and Girls Club of Alachua County, the Alpha Phi Alpha Fraternity, and what I'm most passionate about these days, helping to lead the expansion of 100 Black Men of America to the region. It has been the honor of my life to take part in this work connecting Black professionals with mentoring opportunities to help guide and counsel young men just beginning to make their way in the world.

Gainesville, my adopted home, is an up-and-coming city that, like many cities, demonstrates all of the opportunities available to young Black men as well as the ways they have still been failed and left behind. The same is true across our nation. We know that those critical years of youth can make or break the trajectory of a life. Think about those kids left to fend for themselves studying at home, stuck at home, even more uncertain of the future post-COVID-19 than they were already. We have never needed mentors more urgently than in this moment.

I receive no shortage of satisfaction from my professional endeavors, my community work, and my family. While I'm left with little free time each day, I have a feeling of gratitude for being able to fill each day with so much meaning.

I have long wanted to take some time to put my thoughts down on paper on the challenges and minefields that often have to be navigated by people who, like me, so often find themselves as the only Black person in the room. And yes, this challenge certainly faces women as well! For this book, I am simply drawing heavily from my own experience as a man. There's no doubt that our Black sisters face their own unique hurdles and obstacles that I may never have to consider.

I've written a book before, but I don't necessarily think of myself as wearing an author hat as much as I think of myself as creating a safe space for dialogue, reflection, and hopefully inspiration.

2

CHAPTER 2
Dear White People

M ost Black folks are adept at navigating a world that is rooted in whiteness as a cultural default. The events of 2020 - 2021 have increasingly made it impossible to ignore the very real fractures that exist between Black and White Americans, even when they occupy the same physical space.

For many White Americans, the last years have been a bewildering time. The Trump era normalized the concept of White supremacy from a bully pulpit that was previously unimaginable, even in the era of George Wallace. Few of us will forget the images of White nationalists, not even feeling the need for hoods to cover their faces in secrecy, marching on Charlottesville, Virginia in the summer of 2017.

Many White folks I've personally interacted with—likely not all—find it easy to disavow outright displays of hatred and bigotry. And very few see themselves as racists or harboring overt hatred toward others for the color of their skin. When pressed, they say they are not anti-Black but pro-White. To them, the distinction is important, and provides "cover" for their racism.

The real challenge lies in the inability for deeper reflection. Too many Americans associate the concept of racism with donning a Klan hood and weaponizing the word "nigger," without reflecting on the myriad ways in which our societal institutions themselves remain quietly and deeply rooted in a long legacy of racism and discrimination.

It hasn't been uncommon for me to see yard signs popping up over recent years proudly declaring, "This home STANDS for the National Anthem." It's not enough to fly an American flag at these homes to make their patriotism evident; they must also take thinly disguised potshots at the non-violent NFL protest began in 2016 by San Francisco 49ers quarterback Colin Kaepernick. (I might add, he began kneeling on the advice of a teammate and an ex-Green Beret who recommended kneeling during the National Anthem as a gesture of respect, as opposed to sitting it out altogether.)

Goaded on by the divisive instincts of a president who never missed an opportunity to seize a nativist impulse, many Americans failed to reflect on the connection between peacefully protesting by taking a knee and the military's role in supporting the constitutional right of freedom of speech. Many fixated on the monetary and career success that Kaepernick achieved—before being ostracized by the NFL—and saw a man ungrateful for the bounty his country made possible. By their logic, his own financial success was a validation of the notion that the country worked as promised for anyone willing to work hard.

They failed to consider how Kaepernick's success, like that of many upwardly mobile Black men, compelled him to use what platform and influence he had to lift up the others who hadn't reach the same heights. In Kaepernick's case, his platform just happened to be nationally visible, right before the kickoff of the national pastime. Many viewers at home appeared flabbergasted, unable to make the connection between their Sunday evening entertainment and the disturbing reality playing out across town in communities across America.

Drawing from their own pleasant interactions with law enforcement, White people say,

"Why can't they just cooperate with the police?"

"He had a criminal record. He was no angel."

"If they didn't break the law, they wouldn't have a problem."

These are the familiar rationalizations trotted out time and again as the latest wave of outrage ripples across the nation when the sickeningly familiar story plays out again. Notwithstanding the reality that our justice system doesn't place the decision to prosecute police officers on the beat, when Black people are involved, the charge and subsequent punishment are almost invariably far larger than the crime, when there is a crime at all. A possibly counterfeit twenty-dollar bill, a sale of loose cigarettes, a nighttime walk to the convenience store to buy some iced tea, selling bootleg CDs—none are worth paying the ultimate price of a man's life.

The Reckoning

Some White folks view incidents of police brutality not as appalling systemic racism, but as the actions of a "few bad apples." By their reasoning, slavery ended over 150 years ago. Martin Luther King Jr. awakened the nation's conscience and declared "I have a dream." Americans overwhelmingly elected Barack Hussein Obama to the White House twice in resounding numbers and definitively opened the door to a post-racial society in which children of all colors and creeds could aspire to anything they could imagine.

What they lack is context for just how close we are to this history, only a generation removed from a time when Black people could not legally vote throughout much of the South. It's within our lifetime that interracial marriage was a violation of the law. Loving v. Virginia was the iconic 1967 Supreme Court case that said laws banning interracial marriage violated the Equal Protection and Due Process Clauses of the Fourteenth Amendment to the U.S. Constitution, but the Supreme Court's authority never stretched to the tens of thousands of households that no doubt instituted their own *de facto* bans on their children and family members marrying a partner of another race.

Astonishingly, in March 2022, a US Senator from Indiana, Mike Braun, stated that Loving v. Virginia should never have been decided by the US Supreme Court, and should have been left for each State to decide!

In short, we are still grappling with the grim fallout of periods of our history that were never fully reconciled. The work of reckoning with this past is made doubly hard by leaders who are all too willing to pour gasoline on our discontent to further their own ambitions, and doubly hard in a time when many of us find ourselves communicating far more often via screens than face to face.

And yet this time of lockdown might also hopefully offer more of us the time and space that our busy lives so seldom allow for reflection.

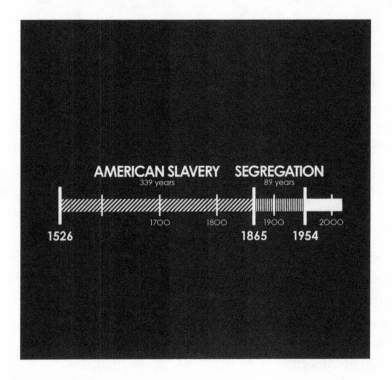

How We Got Here

Many White people I've met seem to view the country's deeply troubled history of racial strife and bigotry through rose-color glasses.

They ignore the reality that we are not so far removed from the time when men who looked like my sons were automatically viewed as rightful property. The last known Black person who had been born into slavery, Peter Mills, died in 1972 at the age of one hundred and eleven years. Just a few generations away—that's how close we are to the cotton fields of the racist plantations that so many of our citizens have written off as ancient history.

That's to say nothing of the dismal steps forward and rapid retreats backwards in the time since. As late as the 1960s in parts of the South, Black women were still denied the right to vote. Our "superstar" advancements in the form of leaders like Vice President Kamala Harris cannot diminish our view that too many Black folks are not beginning their journeys with the same advantages of wealth, status, and especially property rights,` as White Americans, given the restrictions placed on them for far too long well into the mid-20th century, with clear implications remaining today.

We have to remember this long and tortured history for some context to the uprisings we see in Black communities. It's a complete misreading of history to conclude that taking to the streets can't have a tangible impact; as just one example, it took uprisings in cities across America in the wake of the assassination of Dr. Martin Luther King Jr. to finally shame Congress into passing the Fair Housing Act. The act was signed into law just a week after King's murder in Memphis, while Washington and other cities continued to see fires burning in anguished response.

It's little surprise that so many feel as though we have little recourse for driving change in traditional models of politics, dialogue, and negotiation. That has not been the truth of the long Black experience, and it's logical that many find themselves lashing out in dismay over the lack of other avenues to turn to for advancing their concerns.

Yet it's impossible to not look at today's movement and see clear signs of progress. So many of the iconic marches of the 1960s have something in common when you look back on photographs showing almost uniformly Black faces in the crowds assembled. Today's movements, particularly those sparked in 2020 following the death of George Floyd, have been far more diverse in attracting the solidarity and active support of White people, willing to take to the streets and declare that Black Lives Matter.

Many have increasingly woken up to the truth that we continue to live in the shadows of a system that was never fully dismantled. It may well have been a century and a half since White citizens throughout the South were deputized to stop and subdue any Black person they came across; but the hearts and cultural mores of those White citizens were not reversed. In truth, they were barely grappled with. Those laws merely morphed and became new codes of conduct and norms. Black Codes restricted black people's right to own property, conduct business, buy and lease land, and move freely through public spaces. A central element of the Black Codes were vagrancy laws. States criminalized men who were out of work, or who were not working at a job White people recognized. (No points for guessing upon whom these laws were enforced!) It was an early echo of the War on Drugs to come, in which Black and White citizens saw vastly different responses for usage of the same substances.

Consider the present day, when young men can be murdered for walking from a local convenience star with Skittles and iced tea or playing with a toy gun, with their city-paid killers facing no accountability from juries of their peers. It doesn't take a bold historic perspective to see the parallels between the 1930s when White police officers routinely participated in the era's rampant lynching to Officer Derek Chauvin casually pressing his knee into the neck of George Floyd.

And only the most obtuse among us could miss the parallels between the poll taxes instituted in the wake of the 15th Amendment, which in 1870 granted certain qualified Black men (but still no women) the right to vote, and the continued barriers and obstacles placed in the way of Black communities on Election Day today, from onerous requirements for voter identification, to gerrymandering voting districts, to resistance to any efforts to make voting easier through proven, reliable measures like voting by mail. Barack Obama's two terms as President of the United States demonstrated the power of the 1965 Voting Rights Act. But in 2013, The USSC Shelby v Holder that eliminated federal clearance in voting changes provided the justification for Jim-Crow-style voter suppression.

It's heartbreaking to consider the alternative history by which the United States could have played out over the past century and a half if it had followed a course of true reconciliation and justice. The assassination of President Lincoln, and the subsequent elevation to the presidency of the racist Southern sympathizer Andrew Johnson, set this possibility back with catastrophic consequences. The federal government soon reneged on its pledge to grant 40-acre tracts of land to formerly enslaved people in the

South, returning land to traitors and walking away from any meaningful efforts to compensate Black Americans for the horrors that had been visited upon them. Instead, the White power structure merely swapped one form of imprisonment for another in the form of segregation, and, in time, yet another in the form of mass incarceration, as our nation's prison population swelled. In September 2013, the incarceration rate of the United States was the highest in the world at 716 per 100,000 of the national population. While the US represents about 4.4 percent of the world's population, at that time it housed around 22 percent of the world's prisoners—more than even Communist China.

The struggle to live up to our nation's promise rages on. It's a cruel paradox that a nation founded on the precept that "all men are created equal" was established by men comfortable with the notion that in any given state, for purposes of representation in Congress, the total number Black enslaved people should be counted at a rate of three-fifths of that of White people. (Ironically, this formulation gave slave states, which had much larger populations of enslaved Black people than free states, a disproportionally advantageous representation in Congress. Northern states had a higher number of voters, but the 3/5 clause allowed southern states to have more power in Congress.) Waking up to the shakiness of our national foundations on equality is a painful process, one that we have seen playing out in anguished and heated debate, touching on everything from the monuments in our parks and cities to the case for reparations. The dialogue goes on as we grapple collectively with how to best commemorate our history while moving forward with an inclusive vision that creates room for the dreams of all Americans.

The United States was built in no small measure on the sweat and toil of enslaved Black people. Yet so much of this history has been whitewashed and brushed to the side. Look at the example of Nathan "Nearest" Green, a name you may have never heard. Green was a Tennessee enslaved person and the first recognized Black master distiller in America. After the Civil War, he taught young Jack Daniel how to make whiskey. And yet it's not Green's name that has been immortalized on millions of bottles around the world.

In fairness, in 2017 Brown-Forman, the company that owns the Jack Daniel Distillery, made headlines with its decision to finally embrace Green's legacy by significantly changing its distillery tours to emphasize his role and officially recognize Green as its first master distiller. Jack Daniel is now listed as its second master distiller.

The Only Black Man in the Room Syndrome

The challenge to writing this section is how to introduce the philosophical and intellectual discourse from the perspective of Afro-centric and African-American studies. The Only Black Man in the Room syndrome, as I call it, is a result of a White male heteronormative approach to social engagement.

This supremacist dialectic devalues the self-determination and self-evaluative potential of Black thought, skill, and innovation. It's not that Black people are opposed to being in the room, and it's not that we are not interested in integrating. We were, and many still are. However, it's when we are in the room in significant numbers that White males particularly fear losing their self-perceived place of superiority, which in turn fosters their violent responses up to and including murder and rioting—but usually it takes the form of repressive policies couched in bland language.

In modern history, this response has produced the total destruction of towns and Black-inhabited neighborhoods such as Rosewood, Florida. It was there, in 1923, that the world saw the racially motivated massacre of Black people and the destruction of a Black town. The thriving town of Rosewood was utterly destroyed by White supremacist in what would be called a race riot. History tells us that at least six Black people and two White people were killed, though eyewitness accounts suggested a higher death toll of 27 to 150.

The last significant interracial riot was in Detroit in 1943. Today, white rage is expressed through the ballot box and by influencing policies. Witness, for example, the Trump-era wars against "Critical Race Theory," an issue fabricated by racists masquerading as legislators and local school board members.

In other words, being the Only Black Man in the Room has a long history of White supremacists' desire for control over the lives and actions of Black people, because limiting our freedoms and access to power makes them feel safe.

Let me add, however, that while White men are mentioned in the majority of the evidence as the perpetrators of violence, murder, and sexual assault against enslaved people, White women have also played a significant yet underreported role in the subjugation and abuse of enslaved people during the Antebellum period, as well as the most recent uptick of the so-called "Karen syndrome."

In her book entitled *White Women as Slave Owners in the South*, Dr. Stephanie E. Jones-Rogers contends that White women were just as diabolical in their exercise of power over enslaved women as their husbands and other White participants on plantations.

According to an article based on an interview with Jones-Rogers written by Soraya Nadia McDonald, she states, "Not only were White women complicit in acts of sexual violence against enslaved people, but enslaved people also said that there were White women who orchestrated acts of sexual violence against them. A White woman who owned enslaved people in Louisiana would force enslaved men and enslaved women to have sex with each other. When those forced sexual relations produced children, she would keep the girls and sell the boys. And then once those girls came of age and became of age to the point where they could have sex, she would force them to do the same thing. It was a multigenerational cycle of sexual violence that this woman orchestrated."

The above account contends that the girls were kept, and the boys were sold. Therefore, the goal was nothing more than the creation of assets that could be traded on the open market. You kept the females because they could produce more product. The young males were sold, except for a few needed to inseminate the females. I contend that this strategy of selling boys and keeping the girls was one of many abuses that led to, and fostered, The Only Black Man in the Room phenomenon.

Therefore, my critique and analysis of "How we got here" begins with an examination of American racial history and social animus that was fueled and ignited by White supremacy and hatred ever since the days of slavery and Antebellum oppression.

Before 1700, enslaved Black and poor White people often ran away together. Race-based slavery emerged to divide White and Black people. During the first 100 years of British North American conquest, poor White and enslaved Black people were cognizant of their class status. By the late 17th century, Southern states started to pass laws that rationalized race-based slavery.

In October 1669, the Commonwealth of Virginia enacted the Casual Killing Act. This statute made it legal for an officer of a plantation or the master and mistress of a person whom they believed to be an enslaved person to kill such person without impunity. It stated that: "If an Overseer liberally applied violent punishments such as whippings to slaves that they perceived to be transgressive or recalcitrant and if the slave died due to the extreme punishment that the master should not face charges for the murder." This act was put in place to protect against possible felonious charges levied against the punisher.

For the 17th century enslaved person in Virginia, disputes with a master could be brought before a court for judgement. The Virginia Slave Codes of 1705 (formally entitled "An act concerning Servants and Slaves") eliminated this right. An owner who sought to break the most rebellious of enslaved people could now do so, knowing any punishment he inflicted, including death, would not result in even the slightest reprimand.

Many Southern states implemented laws against Black people gathering in groups, and all Black assemblies were to be supervised by some White person. Dating back to Plessy v. Ferguson and the separate but equal statutes, to the burning down of Black towns when Black people asserted their ingenuity, maintaining the number of Black people in a social space prompted White pushback of gargantuan proportions.

James Meredith is a perfect example of the response of White supremacist to the first and only Black man not only in the room but in the entire university.

In 1962, James Meredith, a Black man, attempted to enroll at the all-White University of Mississippi. Chaos broke out on the Ole Miss campus, with riots ending in two dead, hundreds wounded, and many others arrested, ending only after the Kennedy administration called out some 31,000 National Guardsmen and other federal forces to enforce order.

The entire university had to be sequestered because of one Black man's presence. Though the government offered and provided protection while he matriculated, that type of benevolence has long been dismissed from interracial social etiquette.

It is important to highlight that there were, and still are, consequences of being the only Black man in the room. I would argue that we are discussing more than a Black man in the room. We are actually highlighting the fear of the Black man being *anywhere*. To this day, we see a concerted effort by the dominant White male heteronormative culture to prevent diversity and inclusion on the part of Black people in general and Black men in particular.

Here are just a few examples, ripped from the headlines:

On August 23, 2020, Jacob S. Blake a 29-year-old Black man and father, was shot in the back while entering his SUV. Officer Rusten Sheskey, a seven-year veteran of the Kenosha Police Force, held Blake's undershirt while he shot him in the back. Seven shots were fired, four of which entered Blake's body. As a result, Blake was paralyzed from the waist down.

On May 25, 2020, George Floyd, a 46-year-old Black man, was murdered by a White Minneapolis police officer named Derek Chauvin.

The police were called because Floyd had allegedly passed a counterfeit twenty-dollar bill at a local store. Officer Chauvin pressed his knee on Floyd's larynx, causing him to cry out "I can't breathe" for a total of 8 minutes and 46 seconds. This occurred while three other officers stood by and offered no assistance to Floyd. He was literally suffocated in full view of bystanders and not one person in uniform offered to assist Floyd. Officers J. Alexander Kueng and Thomas Lane further restrained Floyd, while officer Tou Thao prevented bystanders from intervening.

On February 23, 2020, Ahmad Marquez Arbury, an unarmed 25-year-old man, was pursued and fatally shot while jogging near Brunswick in Glynn County, Georgia by Travis McMichael and his father Gregory, who were armed and following him in their pickup truck.

The murders mentioned above are only a sample of the diabolical nature of maintaining the Only Black Man syndrome. We have seen over the centuries that Black men and women can be killed with impunity, and I assert that the underlying reason is what I've referred to as the only Black man syndrome.

Just as the owners of enslaved people in the 19th century were granted immunity if they killed a runaway or a person whom they assumed was rebelling, in today's society, police officers are granted a similar freedom to kill. It's called "qualified immunity." At the Federal level of government, this same process is referred to as "sovereign immunity."

So what, you might ask, does all of this have to do with "How did we get here"?

Have you ever asked why it took so long for the United States to have a president who was not a White man? Have you ever considered that there have been many qualified people of African descent who could have been leaders in the major political parties? The truth of the matter is that ever since Black political expression was crushed during Reconstruction, White men have had a lock on the opportunities of the upper echelon of government.

The title of this book is *The Only Black Man in the Room*. It's more than an acknowledgement, it is an announcement of gargantuan proportions. This book is written specifically to reach out to White people on how it feels to be the only Black man in the room in any professional setting, be it a medical office, corporate boardroom, church—all the way to the Oval Office in the White House. The Only Black Man in the Room syndrome is a product of the fear of losing one's place of supremacy.

It is a reminder that Black men are being killed in the streets of America and prevented from being in the room, and it also highlights the surgical accuracy taken to block our way up the corporate ladders that have often employed those who were less qualified but had the right color skin.

In 1874, only nine years after the end of the Civil War, former enslaved person Blanche Kelso Bruce was elected to the United States Senate as a Republican from Mississippi.

Bruce's predecessor was Hiram Rhodes Revels. One hundred and fifty years ago, on February 25, 1870, visitors in the packed Senate galleries burst into applause as Senator-elect Hiram Revels, a Republican from Mississippi, entered the Chamber to take his oath of office. Those present knew that they were witnessing an event of great historical significance. Revels was about to become the first Black person to serve in the United States Congress. Just 22 days earlier, on February 3, the Fifteenth Amendment to the Constitution was ratified, prohibiting states from disenfranchising voters "on account of race, color, or previous condition of servitude." Revels was indeed "the Fifteenth Amendment in flesh and blood," as his contemporary, the civil rights activist Wendell Phillips, dubbed him.

Senator Revels was the first to be the only Black man in the room. Between 1870 and 1871, the United States elected seven Black men to the Republican House of Representatives: Benjamin S. Turner of Alabama, Robert Carlos De Large of South Carolina, Josiah T. Walls of Florida, Jefferson F. Long of Georgia, Joseph H. Rainey of South Carolina, and

Robert B. Elliot also of South Carolina. My point here is that though Revels, was the first only Black man in the room, it is evident that Black people in the south were not going to make that the norm. Despite there being no evidence that free Black people would seek revenge on their former captors, the fear of Black people gaining political and economic power is what led to the Compromise of 1877, the failed Reconstruction, and the introduction of Jim Crow laws, the origins of voter suppression and the establishment of the Ku Klux Klan as the unofficial terrorist group of law enforcement. These three entities were the primary reasons as to why Black men continue to be the only Black man in the room.

The First Black Members of the U.S. Congress

As such, many White Americans view America's history of racial strife and bigotry with rose-colored lens.

The misconceptions about the devastation caused by slavery, Reconstruction, and Jim Crow are primarily the result of a history of America that has been romanticized. We are expected to forget our past, as if the long-lasting effects of "post traumatic enslaved person syndrome" is of no consequence. It's funny, because no-one asks the Jewish community to forget the Holocaust, and as a matter of fact the

Jewish culture has a tradition that reminds them to "Never Forget." They are said to have long memories, they don't forget their holidays, and they won't and don't want others to forget the Holocaust. It's because the Holocaust was fueled by hatred, and they don't want the world to fall back into that same kind of disdain for another human being or a group of people, and yet there are those who want Black people to forget about the 400-year history of slavery, which was supposed to have ended with the Civil War, as if it were simply a footnote in the development of the United States.

The Emancipation Proclamation, the document authored by President Abraham Lincoln, was supposed to have freed the enslaved Africans. However, in truth it was designed to provide only narrowly defined legal freedom to the 300,000 enslaved Black men and women still being held within the confines of the Confederate states, and in particular to allow Black men to fight for the Union Army while allowing slavery to continue in Confederate areas controlled by the Union Army.

White Americans tend to ignore the reality that we are not so far removed from the time when men and women were considered property and auctioned as commodities in the town square.

In July 2020, Sydney Trent wrote an article in the *Washington Post* entitled: "At 88, he is a historical rarity—the living son of a slave." The article is about Daniel Smith, the son of a former enslaved gentleman by the name of A.B. Smith. According to Daniel Smith, his father "Abram Smith, married a woman who was decades younger and fathered six children. Dan, the fifth, was born in 1932 when Abram was 70. Only one sibling besides Dan — Abe, 92 — is still alive."

The testimony of Daniel Smith reminds us that we are not far removed from slavery, and Jim Crow social constraints. I dare say that if we continue on this present tack, there are those in these United States that are trying to return to the "good ol' days." The truth of the matter is that while slavery is gone, in many ways—especially economically—we're still in the good ol' days.

A recent study on economic disparities reveals that:

Black households in the United States have, on average, considerably less wealth than White households. In 2016, the average wealth of households with a head identifying as Black was $140,000, while the corresponding level for households headed by a White person was $901,000, nearly 6.5 times greater.

One might ask why such a disparity? It's usually connected to opportunity, which further explains The Only Black Man in the Room syndrome. Organizations and companies tend to gravitate toward people who look and behave like the status quo, which usually means if they are "diverse," it's normally to meet a quota and not because diversity is a principle ideal of the organization.

On the other hand, some people realize the power of the only _____ in the room. A recent example of this dilemma is found in the recent tennis tournament cancellation. Let me say first that if we are to advance as a society, we must understand that the recent protests of the murders of George Floyd, Breanna Taylor, Ahmaud Arbery, and many others are just one part of the strategy of overcoming the only Black man in the room, and we can learn that "One Black Woman in the Room" can make a difference as well.

The number one female tennis player in the world, Naomi Osaka, proved the power of one voice. After the police shooting of Jacob Blake in Wisconsin, in a stance for racial justice she announced she would boycott her semifinals match at the Western & Southern Open. Hours later, the U.S. Tennis Association said the tournament would not resume until the following day. Osaka consented to play her semi-final match, which she won.

But it is clear that financial leverage can be a tool of one. Imagine if you will what could or would happen if there were more Black people in the room. I dare say, this is one of the concerns of White leadership.

It helps to understand the root causes of racism among White people, including their leaders. While the subject is vast and complex, it cannot be denied that there are three significant sources of White racism against Black people, which The Only Black Man in the Room cannot avoid or keep from being top of mind:

1. Loss of wealth. This is the belief that all people are tribal and will fight to keep their limited wealth and resources within their own tribes. Therefore, if Black men are given access to financial power, they will use that power to steer opportunities and wealth to "their own kind," thus depriving White people. This is the "slice of the pie" approach, in which the pie is finite, and if you get more, then I must get less. It's related to the fear held by White people that people of color are "stealing our jobs," which happens to be factually untrue, but which has powerful emotional resonance.

2. Retribution. Many White people fear that because they have treated Black people unfairly—even brutally—for the past four hundred years, then if Black Americans gain power, they will turn the tables and do unto White people as the White people have done unto them. Can you imagine being a White racist and imagining a world where the levers of power have been taken out of your hands and given to the people whom you formerly oppressed? It would be a frightening thought. And yet, the historical record indicates such imagined retribution has never occurred.

3. Fear of "The Other." This is the deep-rooted but ultimately irrational belief that someone who *looks* like you is likely to be friendly, while someone who looks *different* may be an enemy. This belief fails to account for the other person's values, which may in fact be closely aligned with yours, regardless of the color of their skin. It helps to know that in fact, the genetic differences between races are amazingly small. "If you ask what percentage of your genes is reflected in your external appearance, the basis by which we talk about race, the answer seems to be in the range of .01 percent," said Dr. Harold P. Freeman, the chief executive, president and director of surgery at North General Hospital in Manhattan, to *The New York Times*. "This is a very, very minimal reflection of your genetic makeup."

Given these emotional obstacles, it's no surprise that so many people feel as though they have little recourse for driving change in traditional models of politics, sports, and other negotiations.

However, groups that seem to be making some headways are the Me Too and Black Lives Matter movements. But many White media execs—especially those in the right-wing media dominated by Fox News—are choosing to distort and mislead the motivation of these movements, especially the BLM. Institutional racism in the established media has been a tool of the dominant culture in preserving their control and place of prominence, and they usually have the resources to maintain this deception, which in turn causes skepticism on the part of their constituents.

The antithesis of this phenomenon of being the Only Black Man in the Room is the American prison system. While Black men have always been imprisoned at a higher rate than White men, from the 1920s to the early 1970s the rate of incarceration remained steady. As recently as 1980, there were only 300,000 federal prisoners. Mass incarceration was not an issue, and in fact many progressives were talking about abolishing prisons. Then, beginning during the Reagan administration and up to the year 2000, the rate of imprisonment in the United States more than quadrupled and the prison population exploded. The vast increase in the prison population consisted of Black men and women.

Today, America has no problem with Black people overloading the prison-industrial complex. Beginning with the Convict Lease System that began just after the Civil War to the school-to-prison pipeline, one would be hard pressed to find only one Black man in an American prison. Though Black people make up less than 13 percent of the total population in America, a recent study on incarceration rates provide astounding statistics on Black to White imprisonment.

Conducted by Ashley Nellis, Ph.D., the study documents the rates of incarceration for White, Black, and Hispanic people in each state, identifies three contributors to racial and ethnic disparities in imprisonment, and provides recommendations for reform. It found that Black people are incarcerated in state prisons at a rate that is 5.1 times the imprisonment of White people. In five states (Iowa, Minnesota, New Jersey, Vermont, and Wisconsin), the disparity is more than 10 to 1.

In twelve states, more than half of the prison population are Black people: Alabama, Delaware, Georgia, Illinois, Louisiana, Maryland, Michigan, Mississippi, New Jersey, North Carolina, South Carolina, and Virginia. Maryland, whose prison population is 72 percent Black, tops the nation.

In eleven states, at least 1 in 20 adult Black males is in prison.

In Oklahoma, the state with the highest overall incarceration rate, of Black people, 1 in 15 Black males ages 18 and older is in prison.

What we know historically about these statistics is that incarceration rates began to increase after the Civil War and during the period of Reconstruction. Southern White people wishing to return to power and to regain control of Black social life instituted Black codes, sets of restrictive laws designed to limit the freedom of Black people and ensure their availability as a cheap labor force.

For example, under Black codes, many states required Black people to sign yearly labor contracts. If a Black man or woman refused, they were subject to arrest, being fined, and forced into unpaid labor. Northern opposition to Black codes helped undermine support for President Andrew Johnson and the Republican Party.

How could this be? The war was over, and for a short period of time Southern Black people experienced a sense of relief and personhood; but as Michelle Alexander pointed out, this freedom was short lived. Once the White backlash against Reconstruction gathered momentum, Constitutional amendments guaranteeing Black Americans "equal protection of the laws" and the right to vote proved as malleable as the Emancipation Proclamation. Black people found themselves at the mercy of White authorities and relegated to convict leasing camps that were, in many ways, almost as bad as slavery. Hope gave way to despair, and the Jim Crow system of segregation emerged, which returned Black people to a *de facto* subordinate racial caste.

The Only Black Man in the Room syndrome incorporates violence, deceit, power grabs, White supremacy, and hatred. Like racism, it invades every aspect of American society. There is not one area of American social interaction that has not been infected or contaminated with racism and White supremacy.

Elections are a particular concern.

Only the most obtuse among us could miss the parallels between the poll taxes instituted in the wake of the Fifteenth Amendment that granted Black men the right to vote to today's North Carolina Republican Party's attempt at preventing Black voters from getting to the polls by the introduction of the voter-ID laws. From election day shutdowns to gerrymandering, keeping Black people out of the voting booth has been one of the supreme motivations of the modern Republican Party. It has proven to be one of the ways that they maintain the Only Black Man in The Room.

Out of 435 voting members of the U.S. House of Representatives, in 2021 there were only 51 Black representatives and two Black delegates, representing 26 states plus the U.S. Virgin Islands and the District of Columbia.

It's heartbreaking to consider how different United States history could be recorded if over the past century and a half it had followed a course of true reconciliation and justice.

Comedian D.L. Hughley said during an interview that President Obama was what America *could* be, and that Donald Trump was who America *is*. I often wondered if he made that assessment because former President Obama was usually The Only Black Man in the Room?

The Past Remains With Us

Most of us see ourselves as the heroes of our lives. We know the struggles and challenges we have overcome to get to where we are today. That's just as true for White folks. In America, some of the greatest divisions between us are rooted in wealth and class. For lower- to middle-income White Americans still grappling at attempts to stay afloat in a rocky economy, they sure don't feel like they have been the beneficiaries of anything remotely resembling White privilege.

On the contrary, many low-income and otherwise insecure White people see affirmative action programs and diversity initiatives, and conclude that the tables have been turned on them and they are the victims of so-called "reverse racism." Without a box to check on job applications, without a month set aside for their history and heritage, they begin to conclude that the real advantage today goes to people of color.

It's especially true of the downwardly mobile White voters whose support in 2016 pushed Donald Trump over the electoral finish line, and who had concluded that an economy without the guarantee of good manufacturing jobs needed a stark jolt to the system, even if it came from a reality TV star who rose to political prominence promulgating the racist fantasy that the first duly elected Black president had been born overseas and needed to show his papers, an indignity never before demanded of any commander in chief.

If their whiteness isn't enough to shield them from the economic carnage of jobs being automated and factories closing their doors to high-paying blue-collar jobs, they may then reason that their being White hasn't given them an unfair advantage or leg up in the world.

But even well-meaning White people seldom reflect on the privileges to which they never need give a passing thought. They include the privilege to go shopping without worrying about being suspected of shoplifting, and the privilege of entering a routine police interaction at a traffic stop without considering the probability of arrest, beating, or even death. I can't say that I know what these privileges are like, as moving through the world as a Black man is to grow accustomed to continually watching your back and being prepared to defend your status as a law-abiding citizen.

Virtually every Black father knows the sad ritual of sitting down at some point with his children for "the talk." No, not the "birds and bees" talk, but the discussion of how to behave when interacting with the police. "Make sure they can see your hands at all times," admonishes dad. "No sudden movements. Always smile so they know you're not a threat. Do exactly as they instruct. If you can, make sure you record the interaction on your phone."

This should not be normal. At least, it shouldn't be in a free society. This is a clear sign of a society that has not fully grappled with the full toll that slavery, segregation, and mass incarceration have left on our country. While many of these horrors were corrected in law long ago, their scars linger and leave an impact still today.

It's heartbreaking. We raise our kids and try to get them to hold onto their innocence and sense of wonder about the world for as long as we can. But we quickly find that we can't shield them from the harsh realities that the world will forever be looking at them differently and judging them from a different standard because of the color of their skin.

These are conversations and experiences that White folks don't need to have. An informal sampling of White acquaintances of mine shed light on what we instinctively know: Many of our White friends and neighbors have been conditioned to see the police as a source of safety and security. They don't see any reason to be nervous or apprehensive when having routine interactions with the police. "I haven't done anything wrong, so there is nothing to worry about."

That sentiment is alien to most Black people. It's just one of the most prominent recent examples of how we may inhabit the same physical spaces while living very different realities.

I can seldom go a week without a stray news article catching my eye and only confirming the craziness of the unexpected hoops that Black folks find themselves navigating on an ongoing basis. In December 2018, I saw a story on CNN of an Ohio man who went to his local bank, paycheck in hand from his first week at a new job at an electric company. Paul McCowns wanted to cash the check, and he provided two forms of identification and a fingerprint. Despite following protocol, the teller refused to cash the check. Minutes later, McCowns found himself walking out of the bank in handcuffs and being escorted to the back of a police cruiser, where he was questioned before being released.

The bank teller had called the cops on him. The 911 recording captured it: "I have a customer here—he's not our customer, actually. He's trying to cash a check and the check is fraudulent. It does not match our records."

Such "misunderstandings" and presumptions of guilt are par for the course for Black folks, whether they're simply out birding in their local park or guilty of "driving while Black."

Consider the Miami Gardens, Florida, man who was picked up by police literally dozens of times in a sick twist on "Groundhog Day," all for "trespassing" at the convenience store where *he worked as a clerk.* The store owner, Alex Saleh, was so tired of the constant police harassment that he installed 15 video cameras in his store—*to record the police!* As *The Miami Herald* reported in November 2013, "The videos show, among other things, cops stopping citizens, questioning them, aggressively searching them and arresting them for trespassing when they have permission to be on the premises; officers conducting searches of Saleh's business without search warrants or permission; using what appears to be excessive force on subjects who are clearly not resisting arrest and filing inaccurate police reports in connection with the arrests."

Yes, we are indeed living in very different realities.

The young talented writer Damon Young has called it "nigga neurosis"—the perpetual state that Black folks live in, where we wonder if racism is involved in every little negative thing we experience.

It's just a completely alternative reality altogether. And that is especially true of the place where a lot of us spend the majority of our time, the place where we spend even more of our days than with our family—the workplace.

Navigating Race in the Office

Before the pandemic shuttered office parks from coast to coast, each day in workplaces across the country countless men would don the standard uniforms of corporate America—suit and tie, business casual, casual Friday—and commute to offices where they often found themselves as one of the few faces of color.

The term "minority" has increasingly fallen out of favor and out of step in a country poised to see significant demographic shifts by the middle of the century. But in the halls of investment banks and law firms and countless other professional settings, among the crowds of White faces, Black men remain a distinct minority.

Even when an event like the murder of George Floyd takes place and suddenly launches a new wave of "national conversations" about race, many of us are reluctant to say a whole lot around the water cooler (or in what I suppose is increasingly today's equivalent, the Microsoft Teams chat).

Black employees may be reluctant to play the role of the person whose job it is to help communicate the "Black perspective" to our colleagues. We may just want to do our job, keep our head down, and get in a solid day's pay for a solid day's work. But that is the special burden that many of my Black friends and neighbors bear. It's not enough to be a great salesperson or a great IT developer. We also have to play the role of a racial spokesperson, someone who can help assure our White colleagues that we do live in a colorblind society on the grounds of, "Hey, look at how well we have done."

It's not easy to bear the burden of being a trailblazer, of being a "first." Raphael Bostic, the first Black man to serve as a president of a Federal Reserve regional bank, spoke to *Marketplace* host Kai Ryssdal about what it's like to walk down a long hallway adorned with portraits of his predecessors over the decades, without one bearing any racial resemblance to him.

But the changes that come from a more inclusive and diverse workplace go much deeper than complexion. Bringing Black leaders into organizations where they have never before had the opportunity to lead offers the chance for more voices and more perspectives to be heard. We think about problems in different ways. We have had different life experiences, often that are much closer to the ground level of community problems. Issues like poverty, creating jobs, and environmental degradation aren't abstract to us, but urgent challenges that we have seen devastate our communities.

Just look at the different approach that Bostic has brought to the job compared to those who came before him. The Federal Reserve system has historically been focused primarily on two missions—fighting unemployment and combating inflation. But Bostic, and people who come up with an intuitive understanding of how precariously placed many of our poor communities are, brings a new perspective. Are these really the best indicators for how the economy is doing? Under his leadership, the Atlanta Fed has placed a larger emphasis on addressing economic inequality, driving a more inclusive economy, and looking at ways it can more creatively use the range of monetary tools at its disposal.

That's the real return on investment for more diverse leadership.

The sum total of all of these unique experiences that we bring to the table? We view the world through a different lens than our White colleagues, which can sometimes reinforce the feeling that we are living in different universes, even if we may physically occupy the same space.

Making My Own Way in Corporate America

My story hasn't been one of meteoric ascent, the kind that we sometimes read of distinguished Black leaders in the media. Those can be good stories, but the far more common one is hardly that of an overnight success. On the contrary, the more common story is that of diligently showing up each day, paying one's dues, and continuing to plug away even when the tangible benefits of a reward or recognition seem impossibly far off from fruition.

In my case, I slowly worked my way up over a period of years in the telecommunications industry at the local, regional, and national levels. In time, I continued to grow in responsibility and knowledge until I assumed management roles of increasing levels of responsibility.

I have been blessed and fortunate to spend the majority of my professional career engaged in meaningful work that I care about. I have been empowered to seize opportunities and have met tremendous colleagues along the way. I am aware that my experience may not necessarily be the truth of everyone, but it demonstrates that there is a path to finding meaning and satisfaction in the professional world, even with obstacles stacked against oneself.

As you can speculate, the farther up the ladder I went, and as I participated in high-level meetings and discussions, the more often I found myself the lone Black person in the room.

I don't believe for a moment that the lack of greater diversity was the product of a deliberate or conscious choice to exclude people of color from my workplace. The overwhelming number of my colleagues, superiors, and contacts I have worked with throughout my career have been conscientious, kind, and generous spirited. I have no doubt that most of them would have been pleased to see more diversity in our ranks.

So why wasn't there more? Because the inequities in our leadership pipelines are far bigger than the biases or prejudices of any individual person. These disparities are deeply woven into the very fabric of how we scout, select, and elevate leaders.

Consider the education requirements we have in place for senior positions, which increasingly view education credentials, primarily a college degree from a four-year bricks-and-mortar institution, as table stakes for entry. It's widely assumed that many professional positions must be awarded to someone who has a four-year college degree, regardless of if they studied philosophy or finance; the degree itself is irrelevant compared to the fact that they earned that piece of paper.

I have nothing against pursuing higher education and recognize that there is a level of doggedness and grit that is usually demonstrated by the very act of earning a diploma. But what about the many students unable to cobble together the funding for a traditional college degree?

Access to higher education has improved since my grandfather's time, but it still leaves far too many Black students grappling for straws in a country that has long ago made up its mind to make investing in education a punishing hit to the wallet of the learner. We are still a long way off from seeing higher education as a public investment that benefits all of us.

What about those who, out of fiscal discipline, turn to less prestigious options such as community colleges or online learning, and find themselves essentially shutting themselves out of the managerial track before they have begun the race in earnest?

This emphasis on a certain narrow set of credentials—one that is generally more within reach of White Americans—speaks to the real challenge of bringing more diverse leadership into the fold. Black men often struggle just to get into the pipeline to begin with. Major parts of the value of a college degree are the network it confers and the social cues it instills in students. Studies have demonstrated time and again that applicants with distinctively Black names are far less likely to see follow-up interest in their resumes and applications.

Most of this exclusion, again, is not borne out of any type of intentional malice or ill-intent. On the contrary, it tends to fall into the realm of unconscious bias. We aren't even aware that we are discriminating when we do it. And this reality speaks to the notion of why today's systemic racism may be far more difficult to end than earlier waves. Yes, segregation was an outright horror, but it was a comparatively straightforward process to enforce bans on segregation; what is far more difficult is to break through to the lingering bias that persists with us generations later that continues to drive such unequal outcomes for Black workers.

What can be done? I don't have a silver bullet to offer, sadly. It's a long process. One of the most hopeful trends for me has been the emergence of training specifically focused on unconscious bias in police departments across the country, as local and regional leaders grapple with what can be done to repair the dismal state of relations between the police and the communities they serve.

These proposals remind us that few police officers likely leave their homes in the morning intentionally looking to inflict violence on Black citizens; but their biases and reflexes still lead them to vastly different conclusions when they are interacting with people of color. A similar focus on unconscious bias could make a huge difference in the workplace as well.

These biases are exactly what keep promising job candidates of color from even making it to the first rung on the ladder of advancement. I think of the famous "Rooney rule" that Pittsburgh Steelers owner Dan

Rooney helped to instate across the NFL, requiring that ethnic-minority candidates be interviewed for head coaching and senior positions when vacancies emerge, helping to create a positive expansion in coaching and managerial diversity.

And these proposals are where the conversation gets challenging for many White folks. They think the thumb is placed on the scale in favor of Black candidates, giving them an unfair advantage over their White competitors.

For many White people, it isn't easy to recognize that one has benefitted from a much broader, more insidious form of "White affirmative action" throughout one's life. It isn't easy to concede being given a leg up and walking away from some of that privilege in the name of lifting up others.

> "True integration, true equality, requires a surrendering of advantage."
>
> -NIKOLE HANNAH-JONES.

Not a Colorblind Society

It's easy to think that we live in a colorblind society, in which "may the best person prevail" should be the sentiment with no regard to skin color. But we plainly do not; if our nation had taken steps to fully grapple with the legacy of slavery, segregation, and mass incarceration decades earlier, we might be at a very different moment. But that work seems, to me, to have only just begun in earnest.

In truth, the idea that we live in a colorblind society is the sort of idea that only White folks can entertain, because Black people know the dangers of ignoring race. We can't teach our children they are growing up in a colorblind society, because this could lead them to let their guard down in the workplace or job market. (As President Obama once put it, "…we're also guarding against the subtle impulse to call Johnny back for a job interview but not Jamal.") It could lead them to the mistaken assumption that their innocence will be presumed and their rights will be taken as a given when entering into a routine encounter with a police officer. In short, to teach them that we live in a colorblind society would be to render them ill-prepared to truly face the real society that they are coming of age in today.

It's easy to see the world through a lens of a narrative that we have grown accustomed to: hard work pays off, we all play by the same rules, we should not see color when we look at the world. But these narratives are incompatible with the reality beyond us. It's easy to seek out confirmation of our hunches about the way the world works; Google will offer a cornucopia of voices of high repute and low, eager to confirm what we already think we know about how the world works.

If your working thesis and worldview holds that the Black Lives Matter movement is driven by violent extremists, you can quickly string together the keywords you need to dig up the anecdotal proof points you need to assure you of your position and help you dig your heels in further in the echo chamber on the internet. But this is not a true inquiry for answers or understanding; this is merely defaming the legitimate pain of many by choosing to focus on the outliers.

I think of a cartoon I saw recently in which a young Black man leads a White man on a hike up a mountain. The White man is already winded, bent over with exhaustion. The Black man points impatiently ahead at the path ahead of them. They have passed a sign that reads, "Recognizing Racism in America." Ahead of them, up a steep incline, is another sign: "Doing Something About It."

The Black man crouches over and tells his acquaintance to buckle up for the long climb ahead. "Actually, we're just getting started."

The truth is that if we hope to really understand where we are, then "research" must go beyond reading on the internet. Instead of seeking out information backing up our arguments, consider what could be possible if we devoted ourselves to *listening* (not waiting for our turn to talk) and trying to understand how dramatically different the world can look to others, even those with whom we work each day.

A Man Apart

Medical offices, board rooms, churches, and courtrooms are all places where the average Black professional is continually reminded of his status as "the other", as someone carrying the weight of an entirely different set of experiences. We saw it all the way up to the Situation Room between 2009 and 2017, as a Black commander in chief presided over meetings with military brass and aides in a room of White faces. This perception of standing apart from the crowd has an impact on how you carry yourself and how you interact with your colleagues.

Your mind can find itself drifting to speculating about what is being said about you behind closed doors. Do they really think we are up to the job?

Former First Lady Michelle Obama writes in her book, *Becoming,* of her experience with her first roommate at Princeton, a White girl whose horrified mother demanded they be separated. Even after a lifetime of extraordinary accomplishment and global fame, an incident like this continues to leave a mark. It continues to leave even the highest achievers among us wondering if we will ever fully measure up in the private thoughts of those around us.

I can empathize with the challenges that some White people feel in this moment. Many have come of age and lived most of their lives under unspoken rules that essentially grouped the entire subject of race in with religion and politics as taboo topics not to be discussed openly in polite company. The title of this section itself, "Dear White People" may strike some as needlessly provocative.

Some fear that they don't have the vocabulary or cultural deftness to navigate the so-called national conversation underway. They wonder, "What if I say the wrong thing?" The Language Police are always vigilant. I've seen arguments break out over the internet on social media or blogs when someone asked about the safety of a city neighborhood they described as "up and coming." One person's innocuous statement can unintentionally leave a bitter taste for someone else as a so-called "microaggression"—especially on the internet. What if they post a black square on Instagram with the wrong hashtag, or share a problematic article and set off a war in the comments section of their personal page? Should they capitalize the "B" in "Black" or leave it lower case? Many assess the landmines and conclude that they are better off saying nothing at all.

My hope is that we continue to extend the presumption of good faith to those seeking to learn, listen, understand, and be part of the solution. If that sometimes mean using a term that Black folks find cringe-worthy, let's not use it as an opportunity to "cancel" that person and assume the worst intent. The process of learning and growth can be painful at times; let's commit to helping clear that path for those who are sincerely committed to it.

That said, we are living in a time in America when many of the behaviors that were once considered normal are no longer acceptable. For example, we regularly see stories of leaders on the local level—school board members, mayors, county commissioners—being forced to step down from their posts after sharing racist content online.

Most of us can tell when that fine line has been crossed, and those serving in high positions of public trust should always remember that their public service is a privilege, not an inheritance. Racist jokes, tired stereotypes, hate speech—I'm heartened to see all of these things increasingly called out, especially by the younger generation. If that means not airing old *Saturday Night Live* sketches featuring blackface and setting aside beloved pieces of entertainment that look problematic by today's standards, so be it.

Our culture is dynamic and ever-changing, and time marches on. Our statues of granite don't just reflect the distant past, but who we choose to hold up and emulate in our present. And despite so many of the struggles and all the pain of this moment, I believe there is a real cultural sea change happening around us. This can make for some uncomfortable moments along the path to progress, but some discomfort is a small price to pay for where we can end up as a people.

And let's try to keep perspective: the awkwardness that many White people fear during these conversations pales in comparison to the discomfort that so many Black people have tolerated for many years. Most Black professionals are familiar at some point with being on the receiving end of the so-called "White gaze"—the inscrutable, piercing look from White colleagues that leaves it clearly understood that we are being valued, perceived, assessed, evaluated, and judged as though we were an interloper species introduced into a new environment.

Four Workplace Action Steps

It's difficult to wipe away that gaze with concrete action, even within the most well-intended diversity councils in the world. But there is so much that White people can do in concrete terms if they truly do want to act as allies to the cause in the place where we generally spend the vast majority of our time—in our offices and place of work.

Here are four workplace action steps:

1. Commit to weave a program of diversity and inclusion (call it D&I) into the fabric of everything the organization does on an institutional level. D&I can't be seen as a siloed initiative to be trotted out during specific times of year or in response to flare-ups of racial tensions after the next innocent Black man is murdered by the police. An empowered chief D&I officer needs a seat at the table during all the big discussions to ensure that it's always considered proactively, not as an after-the-fact band-aid.

2. Commit to transparency in data on race in hiring and employment. Make it publicly known the number of people of color in positions of authority, their rates of promotion, and—in a real step toward radical transparency—insight into how their compensation aligns with that of their White colleagues.

3. Commit to tangible actions that can be maintained and sustained long-term, so as to not fall into a routine of "check-box activities" featured in self-serving press statements and marketing communications. When tragedies happen, chief executive officers and business leaders are increasingly expected to weigh in. Perhaps this is a commentary on the low levels of trust the public has placed in elected officials.

Words must be also met with tangible specific actions that fall within the purview of what the company can achieve. When organizations or leaders talk the talk without walking the walk, this is called "performative allyship." In such cases, the words will fall on deaf ears.

4. Think carefully about the representation and image your organizations put forward to the world in terms of who represents your team. Who is the "voice" and "face" of your organization? Does your bench of representatives fully reflect the breadth of diversity in your organization?

None of these are silver bullets or singular solutions to all that ails race relations in America and in the workplace. But they are a start. And a start is what we need.

3

Dear Black Men— and Women

H ey guys.

Facts are facts: you're often going to be the only Black man in the room.

That's why you should *own* it.

Own it in whatever way that means for you. It might mean letting your full authentic self to continue to shine through and not caring if you're worried about what others might make of it.

It might mean drawing from your experiences to identify the parts of your work that you're most passionate about.

However you define yourself and your blackness, figure out how to harness what you love most about yourself and put it to work.

For younger readers, many of you are lucky in that you have grown up in a world where a range of possibilities for your life may likely seem open to you, no matter the color of your skin. That wasn't true for a lot of us older folks. When we were growing up, we often had to look far and wide to see people who looked like us represented on television or featured on a magazine cover.

Looking to Role Models

Ever since the days of Crispus Attucks—considered to be the first Black Patriot because he was killed in the Boston Massacre in 1770— each generation has its heroes. In my life, I have been fortunate that I have always found role models and mentors. I often think of specific individuals who modeled to me the full range of what I could aspire to. Thanks to role models such as my grandfather, the door was kicked in a bit more to the next generation, to folks like my mother, the first in our family to earn a college degree, which was an extraordinary achievement in our family. She went on to live her dream and a career as an educator for special needs children. And she raised two Black men to be resilient and ready for life's challenges.

My brother Christopher overcame incredible odds growing up in the 1990s, the height of the so-called War on Drugs, which so often looked more like a War on Young Black Men. He persisted, as he had more than a little of my grandfather and mother's spirit in him. Just as they had their own tribulations to face in the 1920s and 1960s, he faced his own obstacles in the 1990s, just as you will face your own throughout the 2020s.

As the author Ta-Nehisi Coates wrote, "No matter what the professional talkers tell you, I never met a Black boy who wanted to fail."

My brother went on to law school and became a state director for the Louisiana Department of Justice.

What I want you to know is that these individuals are no more special than you. They are no more capable. They have no superpowers that you don't possess. What they shared was a determination and a sense that they could succeed. They had the ability, the power, and the skill to face whatever roadblocks life placed in their path.

More than any financial heritance, that is the great gift that they have left for me. As the saying goes, "Legacy is not leaving something *for* people, it is leaving something *with* people."

It is because of their example that I knew I had nothing to be afraid of in this life. I learned that even with the deck stacked against me—as it very often is for Black people, in many ways that persist today—I could not let injustice be an excuse.

It's not enough to rage against the system and just give up. And, I might add, it's not enough to pull yourself up by your bootstraps and look out for yourself. You have an obligation to reach back, and to do your part in correcting the system.

Both of those obligations – doing well for yourself and doing right by your community – require an education, even if it takes some creativity and savvy to make that goal a reality.

Yes, in recent decades we have seen incredible progress across the board. You have opportunities open to you that my grandfather could not have fathomed a century ago. And yet the hard work continues. Dr. King was right when he said that the arc of the moral universe was long; while it may bend toward justice, it is indeed long.

In recent years, we have seen the divisions in our society—particularly between races—exacerbated, especially by irresponsible figures serving in high positions of influence.

The Secrets of the People Who "Do It"

Throughout history, you'll find success stories and inspirational examples of brave people who didn't shrink from the challenge of being the only Black person in the room. They took the odds stacked against them and turned them to opportunities; they recognized what was unique and special about their vantage point and parlayed that into an unpredicted career advantage.

That includes figures from virtually every industry and line of work. It includes everyone from elected officials to business leaders to icons who broke through in the world of sports.

We should be careful to not draw too many conclusions from the examples of some individuals. Having a few examples of Black excellence doesn't excuse us from the work that we need to do to push for systemic change and allow more individuals to make the most of their talents. But we do still need heroes; they nourish us, inspire us, and motivate us to keep going when it seems like we just can't get up to face the fight another day.

As I get older, I am less impressed with those who solely achieve something great for themselves. It is one thing to reach new heights of excellence in business, sports, or the arts; but it is quite another to achieve something great in lifting up others. I find myself inspired by those who reach across divisions and create greater understanding—people like Daryl Davis, a blues musician who spent enormous amounts of time over three decades as the only black man in some very uncomfortable rooms—having dinner and building relationships with members of the Ku Klux Klan.

Most of us would likely find little redeeming or illuminating about looking at the world through the perspective of outright racists; but there are remarkable people like Daryl in the world who can even cultivate empathy for the most mentally sick and depraved of us, and in the process even change hearts and minds. He has made a practice over the years of collecting robes from Klansmen he has hosted in his dining room—emblems of the small dent he has made in the forces of racism simply through the act of breaking bread together.

As Davis told Dwayne Brown from NPR, "The fact that a Klansman and black person could sit down at the same table and enjoy the same music, that was a seed planted. So, what do you do when you plant a seed? You nourish it. That was the impetus for me to write a book. I decided to go around the country and sit down with Klan leaders and Klan members to find out: How can you hate me when you don't even know me?"

It is because of their example that I have learned to not be afraid of new challenges myself.

Like when I became an author for the first time. Writing can be a tough slog, with a lot of lonely hours spent with your butt in a seat. The end result was my first book, *Dream It. Plan It. Do It.* My goal with the book was to leave the reader with something very actionable… a road map that they could come away with and begin implementing, begin putting into motion, in order to achieve their goals in life, whatever those might be.

In the book, I discussed 50 characteristics that set successful people apart and indicate a person who is truly "doing it."

That list inspired me to think about another list, one of the words of advice and counsel I would give to a young Black person beginning to make their way in the world of work.

Of course, depending on your industry, title, goals, and so on, there are many exceptions and considerations to factor in. And yet I find so often when I meet other professionals, whether at a conference or at an airport bar or anywhere else, we seem to encounter similar hurdles. So take my advice with a grain of salt, but I'm confident that you will encounter similar challenges at some point along the way. This advice can help you, at the very least, learn from the benefit of the mistakes that I have made, rather than having to go out and make those mistakes yourself.

It's important to pass on what we have learned to others. Too often we get caught up in our own pursuit of success and forget to bring others along with us. Yes, we all need to make a living. We have bills to pay and tuition is still far too expensive at too many institutions in this country—a challenge that hits Black families especially hard.

But to focus your life solely on making a quick buck is, I would submit, not worthy of your efforts and talents. Throughout the course of your education, you are going to be putting in a lot of work. Life can become quite a slog if your only consolation is money.

Sometimes you may find that your professional journey has led you astray from your core passions and motivating principles. I urge you to remember that life is too short for work in which you can't find the meaning. Every job will have mundane aspects and tough days, even tough years and decades. But don't settle for a life of misery for a paycheck.

Try to find a cause bigger than yourself. Find a mission that excites you and propels you out of bed in the morning. No, we don't all have the luxury of spending our careers in our dream job, especially in those early years when we're gaining experience. But we can all find ways to use our skills to give back and to serve others.

I don't aim to sound like I'm preaching; but I know what a difference it has made in my life to be able to find clear ways to connect my vocation with my purpose.

Are you good at numbers? Headed for Wall Street? Good for you—but you may also look at ways you can help others to save, invest wisely, and build wealth. Use your skills to give back to others.

Headed for medical school? Wonderful ambition—but you can make time to use your gifts in a free clinic or on a medical trip.

There are infinite ways to leave your mark and leave the world a little better through your gifts.

Allow me to humbly offer some suggestions based on my own meandering experiences. The beauty of advice—even when unsolicited—is that it offers the potential to learn from the mistakes of others, without having to endure the pain yourself!

The Black Man in the Oval Office

I remember reading the memoir of a Black man, in which he wrote about how much he drifted without purpose during his first two years at Occidental College in California. School came fairly naturally to him, but he was more interested in partying, so he mostly coasted. He had only chosen Occidental in the first place to chase a girl he had met while she was on vacation in his native state of Hawaii. He drank and smoked too much. Spent more time playing basketball than hitting the books. He was hardly seen as a rising star.

And yet, college slowly broadened his horizons. He began to get interested in politics, in the divestment campaign that was fighting apartheid in South Africa. He slowly became a campus activist, grew comfortable speaking in front of crowds, and found his voice.

That student who lacked direction became the 44th President of the United States, and launched the national My Brother's Keeper initiative, devoted to connecting young black men across the nation with mentors taking on active, long-term roles in their lives.

Thanks to Barack Hussein Obama, millions of young people grew up in a world where they took it as a given that the president could be a Black man. They grew up hearing President Obama's familiar voice in the background, on the TV. You might not appreciate how unthinkable this once seemed! Many of your parents and many people my age never thought we would live to see the day.

As Nelson Mandela said, "Anything seems impossible until it is done."

When I was young, my mother had a book that showcased famous Black people from throughout history featured on postage stamps.... King, Parks, Owens, Rustin, Tubman. (Some names you may not know yet, but you will.) Icons, giants. They seemed fixed in history, like gods.

But today, in the fullness of time, I understand they were flesh and blood people. They had the same flaws, the same foibles as anyone. And just as they blazed a trail forward, so can we, in our own time.

Think of what seems impossible to you, and what aspiration seems out of your reach. Let me tell you—when you look back on it later, it will seem so inevitable.

I think we're just getting started. Something has fundamentally shifted in our culture. Much of it could have to do with technology; with a cell phone in every pocket, it is harder and harder for blatant racism and oppression to be swept under the rug. The Civil Rights Movement became real for many Americans only when they saw the images of oppression on TV, when they saw police dogs attacking young black men throughout the South in places like Selma and Birmingham.

What has changed today is that we won't allow our outrage to be drowned out by the media. We each have a voice, and all of us can take a stand against bigotry and racism. Not only in individual hearts, but in our institutions and power structures.

"Twice as Good"

It's sometimes said that to get ahead, Black men have to be twice as good.

It isn't enough to work hard and excel at your craft; you are also expected to be an example and a role model, and to blaze the path forward for those who come after you.

I think we are just getting started. This generation is not going to settle for anything less than our very best. We're not going to accept a system that tilts against us. I know we are going to see a lot of trailblazers in the years ahead, and Black people who fly higher than those who came before. As Michael Eric Dyson, a noted Georgetown professor of African-American Studies, said on a Tavis Smiley Black Agenda Forum, "President Obama is Jackie Robinson. I'm waiting for Willie Mays to come behind him, because Willie's got a helluva swing!"

I wish for you, in the years ahead, the courage to follow your interests and your passions wherever they may lead, even if you find yourself in some unexpected places. Remember, Barack Obama didn't go to college to groom himself for politics; he found his passion by opening his mind up to possibilities, by engaging with others, and by being an active part of the community.

Think of the countless rooms he had to stand alone as the only Black man in the room. – from college seminars at Columbia University to fancy fundraisers to the U.S. Senate itself, where he was the lone African-American when elected in 2004, and only the third to serve in "the world's greatest deliberative body" – perhaps not the most apt term - since Reconstruction. (He has since been followed by another 6, including future Vice President Kamala Harris.)

Think of the upside of what that experience can do. Yes, it's challenging to stand apart; but it can also steel you. You're thrown into the deep end. You have no choice but to learn to engage with and build connections with people who don't look like you. And ultimately, all of us must learn to operate in a world in which we will always stand apart in the eyes of some.

I hope you will lose yourself in the pursuit of your passions—and even ones you may not even recognize yet.

"At my first boardroom meeting, there wasn't a seat for me at the table full of white men, so I asked the CEO to move over."

-Jackie Nelson

4

OBMIR
Success Stories

Too often, we get so wrapped up in focusing on the challenges we face that we forget to celebrate those Black men who have gone before us, and who, by their dedication, perseverance, and sometimes even brilliance, have achieved greatness within the White system.

I'm not talking about the many Black Comets who shoot across the sky, visible to all. We rightfully celebrate well-known sports figures such as Jackie Robinson, Hank Aaron, and Michael Jordan; entertainers including Sidney Poitier, Morgan Freeman, and Tyler Perry; and of course high-profile politicians such as Barack Obama, Eric Holder, and General Colin Powell. But most of us are not athletes, actors, or potential presidents of the United States. Like our brothers and sisters of all races and ethnicities, most Black men are not shining comets, high in the sky. They are instead engaged in the everyday, humble tasks of supporting their families, contributing to their communities, and earning a living in business, either as entrepreneurs or within corporate America.

In this chapter I'd like to shine a spotlight on some amazing and accomplished Black men whose names you might not know; but for that very reason, their stories of success might be more relatable. Upon reading them, you might respond by thinking, "Hey, if he can do that, I bet I can do it too!" If there are times you feel that as the OBMIR, you are like a pioneer, exploring unknown territory, then these stories may give you confidence in knowing that you are not alone.

Eugene Parker

Many people—especially fans of pro football—know the names Deion Sanders, Emmitt Smith, and Larry Fitzgerald. These men, and many more, are known not only for their prowess on the field but also for their lucrative deals with their NFL teams. NFL owners are not in the habit of handing over huge sums of money to just anybody, and it takes a special kind of person to get the best deals for the top players.

What set these players apart from the crowd was the first successful Black sports agent—Eugene Parker.

The NFL has been known for being Black on the field and White in the back office. On the gridiron, roughly 70% of the players are Black, but in the league's offices this number plummets to about 10 percent, and of team CEOs and presidents, the number is zero. As Sportscasting. com said, "It's not uncommon for NFL players to refer to the NFL owners as members of a 'rich white boys' club.'" As of 2021, there's not a single NFL team owned by a Black man. Only two people of color own NFL teams: Kim Pegula, a woman of South Korean descent, co-owns the Buffalo Bills. The other NFL owner of color is Shahid Rafiq Khan, a Pakistani-born American, who owns the Jaguars. Every other NFL owner is white.

Sports agents play a critically important role in the NFL and other leagues. An NFL agent does more than just negotiate a deal for his or her client. They're responsible for the daily tasks of advising and managing the careers of the athletes they represent. Besides attending to their clients' professional and personal issues, they must also promote their clients to potential business partners.

Success leads to more success—a sports agent who helps their client obtain lucrative appearance fees and endorsement deals, and make the right career moves, will attract other clients, and be on their way to building a profitable career.

For decades, the NFL sports agent industry was exclusively White male. It was a closed shop. In many ways, it still is, especially for women. According to *Sports Business Journal*, as of June 2020, there were 800 NFL Players Association-certified agents. Of those, only 34 were women—equating to less than 5 percent.

For Black sports agents, change is coming. As Robert Klemko reported for *The Washington Post* in April 2020, NFL agent Nicole Lynn—who made history as the first Black woman to represent a top-five NFL draft pick—woke up the morning after the first round of the NFL draft and thought to herself that at the draft there seemed to be an unusual number of players represented by Black agents. She started making a list, and she realized her impression was correct: For the first time in NFL history, more than half of the players selected in the first round of the draft were represented by Black agents.

As Black agent David Mulugheta, who led the list with four first-rounders, said, "I don't think families [of young athletes] entertained having an African-American agent for a long time.... People look at a young black kid and think, 'What can he really do for me?' I still get that to this day, to be honest with you, and I've been in the business for a while. I think you have a lot of players now who feel they don't have to go with the status quo."

At one time, NFL agents were all White. The first successful Black agent, and the man who at one time was the OBMIR at the NFL draft, was Eugene Parker.

Born and raised in Fort Wayne, Indiana, Parker attended Purdue University, where he studied business management. He was also a four-year starter on the Purdue men's basketball team, and was a team captain for two years, during which he earned all-Big Ten awards and the John

Wooden Award as the Boilermakers' Most Valuable Player. After his college career, Parker was drafted in the late rounds of the NBA draft by the San Antonio Spurs, but he turned down the offer to take a graduate assist coaching job at Valparaiso University while he earned a law degree at the Valparaiso University School of Law.

At the time of his graduation in 1982, Parker had put together a potent three-pronged combination of skills: He was a top-level athlete, and he had degrees in both business management and law.

Parker then started his company, Parker & Associates, which he later re-branded as Maximum Sports Management. His early signings included NFL All-Pro defensive players Rod Woodson and Deion Sanders. In 1995, Parker negotiated Deion Sanders' lucrative seven-year, $35 million contract, with a $13 million signing bonus, which at the time was highest signing bonus in history and made Sanders the highest paid defensive player in the NFL.

In 2005, *Black Enterprise* magazine named Parker one of the 50 most powerful African-Americans in sports.

On August 6, 2011, Parker became one of only four sports agents to ever present a player into the National Football Hall of Fame when he ushered his long-time client and friend Deion Sanders into the 2011 Pro Football Hall of Fame.

He served as partner and agent for Relativity Football, representing roughly 30 active clients including Larry Fitzgerald, Jason Pierre-Paul and three of the top seven picks in the 2015 NFL draft.

Tragically, in 2016 he died of kidney cancer at the age of sixty.

"Eugene and I were more than business partners, we were brothers," vice president of Relativity Sports and agent Roosevelt Barnes said in a statement. "I have known him since I was eight years old in Fort Wayne. Eugene was one of the smartest and most innovative people in the sports business. He handled everything with grace and humility. His imprint on the NFL and the men who played the game will be felt for many years to come. He will be profoundly missed."

Arnold Donald

How about a quick show of hands: How many of you associate the cruise industry with Black people? And I don't mean the people who change the beds and serve the food, I mean the people who own and control the big cruise lines—Carnival Corporation, Royal Caribbean Group, NCLH-Norwegian, MSC, and Disney.

It's a massive industry, with 2017 revenues of $37.8 billion, and with post-pandemic growth expected to hit $57 billion in 2027.

Historically, it was traditionally a White industry, with White owners and White patrons. As Michael Bennett wrote in "The Cruise Industry and The African-American Traveler," when he took a cruise in 1987 on the *Carnival Princess*, "It was three days before I realized there were only three African-Americans on a ship that easily held 2,500 people including the crew.... It troubled me for weeks. It certainly couldn't have been for lack of awareness about cruising."

That's changing. Today, some cruise lines, perhaps having realized that Black cash is just as green as White cash, and that Black passengers don't have cooties, are marketing themselves to Black consumers. For example, in the first decade of the 21st century, Royal Caribbean created the position of director of multicultural markets, which launched a fully integrated ad campaign targeting African-Americans. Their national print campaign targeted Black lifestyle and travel by advertising in such publications as *Essence* and *Ebony*. The company also forged partnerships with television outlets TV-One, BET-J and WGN, the Chicago-based superstation with a nationwide audience, as well as targeting the meetings market through an advertising program in *Black Meetings & Tourism*.

Carnival Cruise Corporation is the biggest player—with over 100 ships, its subsidiaries include AIDA Cruises, Carnival Cruise Line, Costa Cruises, P&O Cruises, P&O Cruises Australia, Cunard, Princess Cruises, Holland America Line, and Seabourn.

Since July 2013, the CEO of Carnival Cruise Corporation has been Arnold Donald. The former CEO of Monsanto, he was summoned out of retirement when Carnival was facing two serious challenges: the 2012 Costa Concordia tragedy and the 2013 Carnival Triumph engine fire. Under his stewardship, until the pandemic—which kept the entire industry tied up at the docks—the company showed steady growth. Total revenues for the full year 2019 were $20.8 billion—a new record, and higher than $18.9 billion for the full year 2018.

From an early age, Arnold Donald planned for his success with unmatched clarity and determination. Born in 1954 into the poverty-stricken, crime-ridden 9th Ward of New Orleans, by the time he reached junior high school, his parents saw his potential and enrolled him at St. Augustine, an all-male, all-Black Catholic high school in New Orleans. Every day, three times a day, the school blasted this message through its PA system: "Gentlemen, prepare yourselves! You're going to run the world!" (At an all-White school, such a message would be alarmingly creepy, but at St. Augustine it served as good and necessary fortification against the racial climate of the Deep South in the late 1960s!)

Reflecting on the school's intense focus on personal success, Donald told FOX Business, "My high school drilled that in me, as well as my parents, even though society around me was telling me you're a second-class citizen. It instilled in me the belief that anything is possible."

Filled with confidence, at age 16, Donald decided that he was going to be a general manager at a Fortune 50 science-based global company. To reach his goal, he created a career plan.

"I mapped it my junior year in high school and I kept mapping throughout college," the CEO told *CNBC Make It*. "I said, 'I'm going to have to have an MBA, a business degree.'" To prepare, he chose to major in engineering at Washington University. But that wasn't enough—he decided that having *two* undergraduate degrees would make him stand out from the crowd. He then pursued an economics degree at Carleton College in Minnesota.

Armed with his two degrees, he enrolled at University of Chicago Booth School of Business.

"I mapped it out," he said. "I had a whole career plan and then I executed it."

In 1980, with a fistful of lucrative job offers, he accepted a position at Monsanto, the Missouri-based agricultural biotech company, where he quickly moved up the ladder. At the age of 32, Donald was named general manager, achieving the goal he had set when he was in high school. Then, after a stint as CEO and chairman at Merisant, the makers of artificial sweeteners Equal and Canderel, as well as natural sweeteners PureVia and Whole Earth, he retired. He was 51 years old.

In 2013, Carnival Corporation called him out of retirement.

"I did hesitate because I was retired and on boards," he told FOX Business. "I wasn't sure I wanted to get back to the pace. But this is just an insanely fun, interesting, exciting, and high human spirit level business."

Donald's performance as CEO didn't go unnoticed. CNBC's "Mad Money" host Jim Cramer called him "the man who may be the best turnaround artist of our time." But Donald says that his rise to the top of Carnival's cruising empire was simply a matter of internalizing St. Augustine's call nearly 50 years earlier. "If you prepare and [have] no excuses, you can pretty much do whatever you want."

Octavius Valentine Catto

Some heroes are celebrated in their lifetime and then forgotten by history, until an event or cultural shift provokes a revival of their memory and a new appreciation for their achievements and the price they paid.

As we turn the corner on yet another presidential election, marred (again) by evidence of the attempted suppression of the Black vote by the conservative party as it desperately clings to power, we are reminded of the sacrifices made by those brave Black men and women who have gone before us.

Octavius Valentine Catto was one of those rare Black Americans who, in the years before Emancipation, was born a free man. But rather than dedicate his life solely to his own self-preservation or prosperity, he lived a life of service to others – and in the process, blazed a path for so many of the only Black Men in the Room to follow in the generations ahead.

When he came into this world on February 22, 1839, his mother, Sarah Isabella Cain, was a member of Philadelphia's prominent mixed-race DeReef family, which had been free for decades and, as a mark of their status, belonged to the Brown Fellowship Society. Founded in Charleston, South Carolina in 1790 by five free non-White people who attended St. Philip's Episcopal Church, the goal of the Society was "to provide benefits which the white church denied them, like a proper burial ground, widow and orphan care, and assistance in times of sickness." Those who joined the club considered themselves "brown" or mulatto, an important distinction at the time when society in Charleston recognized three races: White, Mulatto, and Negro, including octoroons and quadroons. "Pure" Black people were denied admission to the Brown Fellowship Club. (Yes, it was a complicated period in history.)

Catto's father, William T. Catto, had been enslaved in South Carolina, and had gained his freedom. He was ordained as a Presbyterian minister before taking his family to the free state of Pennsylvania, which had officially, but not entirely, abolished slavery in 1780. (Again, it was complicated.)

Catto did well in school. In 1854, he became a student at Philadelphia's Institute for Colored Youth (ICY). Managed by the Society of Friends (Quakers), the curriculum included classical study of Latin, Greek, geometry, and trigonometry. There he presented papers and took part in scholarly discussions. He graduated from ICY in 1858, followed by a year of post-graduate study, including private tutoring in both Greek and Latin, in Washington, D.C. Returning to Philadelphia, among his many other civic and professional activities, he served as teacher and then principal at ICY until his death in 1871.

During the Civil War, Catto was active in the recruitment effort, and helped raise eleven regiments of United States Colored Troops in the Philadelphia area. Catto himself was commissioned as a major, but did not fight. (In those days—unlike today—you could buy yourself a military commission, or be granted one.)

After the war, among other causes, Catto fought tirelessly for the desegregation of Philadelphia's trolley car system. He was instrumental in the eventual passage of a Pennsylvania law prohibiting segregation on transit systems in the state. His crusade for equal rights hit a high mark in March 1869, when Pennsylvania voted to ratify the 15th Amendment, which effectively provided the right to vote to black men. (No women then had the vote.)

In addition to his work as a scholar and civil rights activist, Catto was also an accomplished baseball player, helping to establish Philadelphia as a center of Negro League baseball.

Like so many Black men before him and after him, Catto's life was brutally cut short.

In 1870, Black Americans voted for the first time in Philadelphia, and they elected a slate of Republican candidates. During the following year's election, White Democrats were determined to keep Black people from voting.

On Election Day, October 10, 1871, fights broke out in the city between Black and White voters, as the elections were tense and the two parties—Republican and Democratic—were set in racial opposition. On his way to vote, Catto was intermittently harassed by White Democrats. At the intersection of Ninth and South streets, Catto was accosted by Frank Kelly, who shot him three times and killed him.

By an all-white jury, Kelly was convicted of neither assault nor murder.

Catto's murder caused a national uproar. *The New National Era*, a newspaper published in Washington and edited by Frederick Douglass, the civil rights activist and abolitionist, called Catto a martyr: "His death will not have been in vain," the newspaper said, "if it rouses the people of this city and country of a more earnest determination to protect citizens of every class and color in the exercise of a citizen's most sacred right—the right to vote as his conscience directs him."

His memory quickly passed into obscurity, seemingly to be forgotten.

But in 2016, to honor the man whom many had begun to call the "19th century Martin Luther King," Philadelphia mayor Jim Kenney announced that a new sculpture to commemorate Catto and other leaders would be erected outside Philadelphia City Hall.

The sculptural group, *A Quest for Parity*, which included a twelve-foot bronze statue of Catto, was dedicated at Philadelphia's City Hall on September 26, 2017. Bronze plaques and inscriptions on the surrounding pillars describe Catto's life and inform viewers about how his accomplishments reshaped Philadelphia. Created by Black sculptor Branly Cadet, the work was the first public monument in Philadelphia to honor a specific Black American.

Guion S. Bluford, Jr.

On April 12, 1961, Yuri Gagarin, from the Soviet Union, became the first person to ride a rocket into outer space and return safely to Earth.

Less than a month later, on May 5, the United States put Alan Shepard into a Mercury capsule, put the capsule on top of a Redstone rocket, and blasted him into space. Fifteen minutes and 22 seconds later, he splashed down in the North Atlantic Ocean.

The space race was on!

At this time, a young man named Guion Bluford was a college student at Pennsylvania State University, where he was studying aerospace engineering. Born in 1942 in Philadelphia, he had attended Overbrook High School, a public school known for producing a disproportionate number of famous alumni, including Negro baseball league star Bill Cash, basketball star Wilt Chamberlain, and actor Will Smith.

Bluford received his Bachelor of Science degree in 1964, and then earned his Master of Science degree in aerospace engineering from the US Air Force Institute of Technology (AFIT) in 1974. That wasn't enough; in 1978 he earned a Doctor of Philosophy degree in aerospace engineering with a minor in laser physics, again from AFIT, and then a Master of Business Administration degree from the University of Houston–Clear Lake in 1987.

Whew! That's a lot of degrees!

Meanwhile, he pursued a career in the US Air Force. In 1966 he attended pilot training at Williams Air Force Base, and then went to F-4C combat crew training in Arizona and Florida before being assigned to the 557th Flying Training Squadron.

It wasn't easy being a Black airman. While President Harry S. Truman's Executive Order 9981, issued on July 26, 1948, had officially abolished discrimination in the military, real life was very different. In many ways, it still is. Lieutenant General Anthony J. Cotton is the first Black three-star deputy commander of Air Force Global Strike Command. In July 2020, he told reporter Rachel S. Cohen for her article, "Black Airmen Talk Race in the Air Force," that even with his rank, he's seen too many police lights flash in his rearview mirror, has needed to convince people he was a wing commander, and has been told not to park in his own spot among spaces reserved for base leadership. He has explained to others, she wrote, over and over, what it's like to be Black in America. He wants people to listen. He wants them to get uncomfortable. He wants them to act.

"Here I am as a lieutenant general in the United States Air Force, but … I have a common bond," he told Cohen. "When I see what happened to Ahmaud Arbery, Breonna Taylor, George Floyd, Rayshard Brooks—and the list goes on and on—it's visceral to me. That could be my son. That could be my daughter. That could be *me*."

Guion Bluford served as a T-38A instructor pilot, a standardization/evaluation officer, and as an assistant flight commander. In early 1971, he attended Squadron Officer School, and then in August 1972, he entered the USAir Force Institute of Technology residency school at Wright-Patterson Air Force Base, Ohio. Upon graduating in 1974 with his master's degree, he was assigned to the Air Force Flight Dynamics Laboratory at Wright-Patterson Air Force Base as a staff development engineer. He served as deputy for advanced concepts for the Aeromechanics Division and as branch chief of the Aerodynamics and Air frame Branch in the Laboratory. He has written and presented several scientific papers in the area of computational fluid dynamics.

In January 1978, Bluford was selected to become a NASA astronaut in training, which he and his group completed in August 1979.

On August 30, 1983, Bluford's first space mission was on the space shuttle *Challenger*, which launched from Kennedy Space Center, Florida. This flight made him the very first Black American astronaut to be sent into space. (Three years earlier, the Soviet Union had sent Tamayo Méndez, a Cuban of African descent, up to the *Salyut 6* space station. No doubt this increased the pressure on NASA to send a Black American into space.)

The *Challenger* completed 98 orbits of the Earth in 145 hours before landing at Edwards Air Force Base, California, on September 5, 1983.

On October 30, 1985, Bluford again flew into space on the *Challenger*. After completing 111 orbits of the Earth in 169 hours, the space shuttle landed at Edwards Air Force Base on November 6, 1985. This was *Challenger's* ninth and last successful flight.

In 1991, Bluford flew again into space on the *Discovery*. His fourth and last flight was also on the *Discovery*, launched on December 2, 1992.

With the completion of his fourth flight, Bluford has logged over 688 hours in space.

Now retired, Bluford can look back on an illustrious career. In 1997, he was inducted into the International Space Hall of Fame; in 2010, the United States Astronaut Hall of Fame; and in 2019, and the National Aviation Hall of Fame. In 2006, Bluford was recognized as a distinguished alumnus of Penn State by being selected as the Grand Marshal for his alma mater's Homecoming celebration.

Josiah T. Walls

When the Civil War ended in April 1865, the nation faced a tremendous challenge: how to "reconstruct" the Union in a way that was ethical and provided equal opportunities to all, but did not further inflame White Southerners, many of whom, especially in the Deep South, simply refused to believe or accept that Black people were entitled to the same rights as White people.

The period we call Reconstruction began fitfully, and then gathered steam after the national elections in November 1866. The subsequent Reconstruction Acts of 1867 divided the South into five military districts and mandated how new state governments, based on manhood suffrage without regard to race, were to be established.

By 1870, all the former Confederate states had been readmitted to the Union, and nearly all were controlled by the anti-slavery Republican Party.

During the following seven years, Black people were elected to public office in unprecedented numbers. Sixteen African-Americans served in Congress during Reconstruction, including Hiram Revels and Blanche K. Bruce in the U.S. Senate; more than 600 in state legislatures; and hundreds more in local offices from sheriff to justice of the peace scattered across the South. The arrival of Black men in positions of political power marked a dramatic break with the country's traditions and aroused bitter hostility from Reconstruction's opponents.

One such Black man was Josiah T. Walls.

Born into slavery in 1842 near Winchester, Virginia, little is known of his childhood. It's possible he was the son of his master, Dr. John Walls, with whom he maintained contact throughout his life.

When the Civil War broke out, he was forced to join the Confederate army and work as the private servant of a Confederate artilleryman. Tens of thousands of Black Americans were compelled to support the Confederate army as cooks, teamsters, laborers, and body servants, with their paychecks going directly to their owners. In 1863, more than 6,000 conscripted Black enslaved people accompanied the 71,000 soldiers of the Army of Northern Virginia into Pennsylvania.

In 1862, at the battle of Yorktown, Walls was captured by the Union Army. The following year he voluntarily joined the United States Colored Troops. This division comprised 175 regiments with more than 178,000 free Black people and freedmen serving during the last two years of the war. By war's end, the men of the USCT made up nearly one-tenth of all Union troops.

Walls rose to the rank of corporal. At the end of the war, he was discharged in Florida and settled in Alachua County, Florida. He became involved in politics and served as a delegate to the state constitutional convention of 1868, representing Alachua County. Later that year, he was elected to the Florida House of Representatives from Alachua County and served in Florida's first Reconstruction Legislature. He then served as state senator for the 1869 and 1870 legislative session.

In 1870, after a contentious party convention, Walls was nominated as the Republican candidate for Florida's sole at-large congressional seat. (Today, Florida is entitled to 27 seats in the US House of Representatives; until 1873, it had just one!) He ran against Democrat Silas L. Niblack, a former owner of enslaved people and Confederate veteran. Walls won the 1870 general election, and on March 4, 1871, was sworn into office.

Niblack contested the results. Nearly two years later, on January 29, 1873, the Republican majority—Walls's own party!—declared Niblack the winner, and Walls was forced out of his seat.

But he landed on his feet. In November 1872, there were now two at-large representatives from Florida to the US Congress, and Walls had won one of the two seats in the 43rd Congress (1873–1875). When Congress convened in December 1873, Walls returned to Washington.

In 1874, Walls ran for re-election to Congress in the newly redistricted 2nd district. He won the election, but Democrat Jesse J. Finley, a former Confederate colonel, contested the results by claiming a variety of supposed irregularities. In a disappointing and disturbing pattern, Finley was eventually declared the winner by the Democratic-controlled House of Representatives.

In November 1876, Walls won a seat in the Florida State Senate, where he championed his cause of compulsory public education.

But Reconstruction was under attack. In December 1865, the first incarnation of the Ku Klux Klan had been founded in Pulaski, Tennessee, and had quickly morphed into a tool of White terror against Black people and freedmen. And the "Black Codes," passed by Southern legislatures, were effectively choking off Black political power.

The Compromise of 1876 effectively ended Reconstruction. The promises of Southern Democrats to protect civil and political rights of Black Americans were abandoned, and the end of federal oversight of Southern affairs led to widespread disenfranchisement of Black voters.

In 1879, Walls left the Florida State Senate. He never again won public office, and he eventually became superintendent of the farm at Florida Normal College (now Florida A&M University).

When he died in Tallahassee on May 15, 1905, he had fallen into such obscurity that no Florida newspaper published his obituary.

Today, we see the echoes of the end of Reconstruction, with widespread and blatant attempts to disenfranchise Black voters. Through gerrymandering and laws that restrict access to the ballot box, White conservative state legislators and governors are seeking to roll back the clock. While since the days of Josiah Walls many battles have been won, the campaign is far from over, and many battles remain.

Robert K. McFerrin, Sr.

Without leaping to unjustified conclusions or assigning blame where none is deserved, I think that most people would agree that historically there has been no doubt that one of the "Whitest" and also most racist cultural institutions in the West has been classical opera.

Long steeped in the concept of European-American cultural supremacy, as an art form opera both glorified White archetypes (kings and queens and such) as well as presented caricatures of Black people (slaves, servants, street urchins). If a Black character was depicted in a featured role, it was routine for White performers to present the role in blackface.

For example, Verdi's *Aida*, considered a masterpiece of the art form, is an opera in four acts. Written by Giuseppe Verdi to an Italian libretto by Antonio Ghislanzoni, and commissioned by Cairo's Khedivial Opera House, it's set in the Old Kingdom of Egypt. It had its première in Cairo on December 24, 1871. *Aida* is the story of an Ethiopian princess—Aïda —held captive in Egypt. She's in love with a general, Radames, and he with her. When he is chosen to lead a war against Ethiopia, we follow the conflict of Aïda's love for both Radames and for her country.

Of course, all the principal characters in *Aïda* have traditionally been played by White singers in blackface (or, as it was called, "traditional dark makeup"). White male composers wrote operas like *Aïda* and *Turandot* for White European singers, but the stories were often set in "exotic" locations. Therefore, makeup was required to make the White performers appear African or Asian. Actual Black or Asian singers were not invited to apply.

For Black performing artists, this "White wall" has been particularly irritating because many Black singers love, and are very good at, the art form itself—that is to say, the glorious singing and soaring melodies of classical opera, which are found in no other theatrical setting. Black performers rightly ask, "Why require White singers to slap on a layer of shoe polish when you could hire highly qualified Black performers to do the same job, without the ridiculous makeup?"

Of course, the answer has been plain old racism.

A notable exception is *Porgy and Bess,* the George Gershwin opera set in South Carolina's Catfish Row. It provides a rare opportunity for Black artists because the Gershwin estate requires that Black actors be cast in all the singing roles. But the copyright expires in 2030, and after that, a company can cast anyone they want.

In 2019, White soprano Tamara Wilson made headlines when she was cast as Aïda at the Arena di Verona, an ancient Roman amphitheater in Piazza Bra, Verona, Italy, that's internationally famous for its large-scale opera performances. After Wilson's first performance, for which she wore dark makeup, which had been a tradition of the production for 106 years, she announced she felt terrible about it and refused to continue to wear it.

Opera is a strange culture, because makeup and fantasy are baked into it. But how far can you go? Reporter Mike Silverman from AP News asked a group of Black opera singers about navigating the industry.

Tichina Vaughn told him about her career in opera, "No path is easy for people of color. Anywhere. Decades ago when I was young and wondering whether should I do this for real, a woman—she was white— told me, 'You need to not think about what color you are.' As soon as you start thinking about yourself as Black, you invite obstacles."

Alfred Walker added, "I kind of had to do that. I go to these foreign countries and I'm singing these roles, and you're the only black man in the room. You look around, there's no one else... I just can't have that as baggage."

In the United States, the crown jewel and guiding light of the opera industry is, and has been, the Metropolitan Opera Company in New York City. Founded in 1883, its first opera house was built on Broadway and 39th Street by a group of wealthy businessmen who wanted their own theater. In addition to the usual racism that you could see on the stage, the company has had a long history of White exclusivity behind the curtain. As Joshua Barone, writing for *The New York Times* in July 2020, pointed out, "The nation's largest opera house—indeed, its largest performing arts organization—paints a telling picture. Its board of 45 has only three Black managing directors. Of the 10 people on its music staff, one is Black; of the 90-member orchestra, two. The Met has presented 306 operas in its 137-year history, none of them by a Black composer."

Black opera singer Morris Robinson commented, "In 20 years, I've never been hired by a Black person; I've never been directed by a Black person; I've never had a Black CEO of a company; I've never had a Black president of the board; I've never had a Black conductor. I don't even have Black stage managers. None, not ever, for 20 years."

If this is the way it is today, imagine how it was back in 1955. In that year, the Met achieved two milestones. One was the hiring of the first Black female singer, the great Marian Anderson, who had a brilliant career in opera until her retirement in 1965. But most people don't know that while Marian Anderson was the first Black singer to perform on the stage of the Met, she was the second Black performer to sign a contract. That honor goes to Robert K. McFerrin, Sr., who signed before Anderson, and who made his debut just a few weeks after Anderson.

His name may be familiar to the reader—he's the father of singer Bobby McFerrin, the highly respected folk-jazz singer who's known for performing and recording as an unaccompanied solo vocal artist.

Robert K. McFerrin, Sr., was born on March 19, 1921, in Marianna, Arkansas. At an early age, he showed vocal talent in his local church's gospel choir. As a teenager he joined two of his siblings in a trio, and they accompanied their father, Reverend McFerrin, on his preaching engagements, singing gospel songs, hymns, and spirituals.

As we see with so many Black achievers, strong parental support and a commitment to education made a big difference. After Robert completed the eighth grade in Memphis, his father sent him to live with his aunt and uncle in St. Louis so he could attend Sumner High School. He joined the school choir and so impressed the director, Wirt Walton, that he began teaching Robert privately. In 1940, McFerrin enrolled at Fisk University in Nashville, Tennessee, and then won a scholarship to attend Chicago Musical College at Roosevelt University. The war interrupted his education, but he returned and received his degree in 1948. Step by step, he built his professional career. Singing as an operatic baritone, his appearances onstage included work with the National Negro Opera Company, which during its existence from 1941 to 1962 was the first Black opera company in the United States.

In 1948, McFerrin moved to New York. In 1956, he sang *Rigoletto*, becoming the first Black in history to sing a title role at the Met. That same year, he was the first Black artist to sing *Rigoletto* in Naples at the San Carlo Opera, and he was also the first Black performer to sing at both the Metropolitan Opera and New York City Opera.

In 1958, for reasons that aren't clear, he left New York to pursue a career in Hollywood. After 15 successful years as a voice teacher, he moved to St. Louis, Missouri, and became artist-in-residence at the St. Louis Institute of Music Conservatory, both performing and teaching. He often sang with his two children, Bobby and Brenda. On November 24, 2006, he died in St. Louis at the age of eighty-five.

George Shirley, the first Black tenor at the Met and, after McFerrin, the second Black male to sing leading roles there, wrote, "Robert McFerrin Sr.'s heart was that of a giant; as one of the world's greatest singers and courageous pioneers, he instilled within me and countless other black males the resolve to pursue our destinies as performers in the profession of grand opera. In spite of the personal hardships he endured, his magnificent voice retained its amazing power and beauty well into his 8th decade..."

One of the lessons we can learn from the very successful McFerrin family is the importance of generational wealth and the ability of children to build upon the foundation provided by their parents. Over the years, our racist society has deployed many institutional tools against Black families, including bank mortgage redlining, to choke off the building of generational wealth. In the future, the necessary improvements to how Black people are treated in America must include equal access to both careers and financial services.

Benjamin O. Davis, Sr.

Most of us are familiar with Colin Powell, the retired four-star general who, from 2001 to 2005, served as the first Black American secretary of state. His illustrious military career culminated in his last military assignment, when on October 1, 1989, President George H.W. Bush named him chairman of the Joint Chiefs of Staff, the highest military position in the Department of Defense. At age 52, he became the youngest officer, and first Black American, to serve in this position.

Until he retired on September 30, 1993, he oversaw the US response to numerous international crises, including the invasion of Panama in 1989 to remove General Manuel Noriega from power and Operation Desert Storm in the 1991 Persian Gulf War. As a consequence of his preference for diplomacy over shooting, Powell earned his nickname, "the reluctant warrior." But he also advocated for the use of overwhelming force when necessary, which he applied to Operation Desert Storm in 1991. His "play to win" approach has been dubbed the "Powell Doctrine."

While during his long career Colin Powell often found himself the only Black man in the room, he wasn't the first Black man to attain the rank of general. That distinction belongs to Benjamin Oliver Davis, Sr.

Born in Washington, D.C. he attended M Street High School in Washington, where he participated in the school's cadet program. Upon graduation, his father, a messenger for the Interior Department, and his mother, a nurse, urged him to enroll in college. Against his parents' wishes, he determined to pursue a military career.

While his official birthdate is July 1, 1877, some sources claim he was born in 1880, and that to allow him to enlist, his parents lied to the Army—a not uncommon practice in those days of neighborhood recordkeeping.

Davis entered the military service on July 13, 1898, as a temporary first lieutenant in the 8th United States Volunteer Infantry (USVI), an all-Black-American unit. This was during the Spanish-American War, when the 7th through the 10th USVIs were designated for Black enlisted men and lieutenants. Company commanders and "field and staff" officers were to be white, a policy that deeply offended Black soldiers. The unit was stationed in Georgia and saw no combat.

At the end of the war, the unit was disbanded. On June 18, 1899, Davis enlisted as a private in Troop I, 9th Cavalry Regiment, one of the original Buffalo Soldier, or all-Black, regiments of the Regular Army. In late 1900, Davis's unit was commanded by Lieutenant Charles Young, the only Black officer serving in the US military at that time. In many ways, his story parallels that of Benjamin Davis.

Born into slavery in 1864, Young had a distinguished military career highlighted by many breakthrough achievements. He was the third Black graduate of the United States Military Academy, despite enduring relentless racism from his fellow cadets.

He was the first Black US national park superintendent (in 1903, the military supervised all national parks), the first Black military attaché, first Black man to achieve the rank of colonel in the United States Army, and the highest-ranking Black officer in the regular army until his death in 1922.

But Colonel Charles Young was never promoted to the rank of brigadier general, a post for which he was well qualified. Why not? Because as the United States was preparing to enter the Great War (we now call it World War I), rumors of his imminent promotion caused a forceful pushback from southern White officers who said they would refuse to be commanded by a Black general. With the approval of President Woodrow Wilson, an active supporter of racial segregation and white supremacy, the War Department solved its problem by removing

Young from active duty, claiming it was due to his high blood pressure. On June 22, 1917, Young was placed temporarily on the inactive list, with the rank of colonel.

In 1919, Young was reassigned as military attaché to Liberia. Two years later, in Nigeria, he fell ill, and died of a kidney infection at the British hospital in Lagos on January 8, 1922. He was only 57 years old.

Meanwhile, Benjamin Davis was dutifully climbing up the ranks. He served in Liberia, and then was ordered to patrol the Mexican-United States border. In 1915, he was assigned to Wilberforce College as professor of military science and tactics. Then the Army sent him to the Philippine Islands, and in 1920 he returned to the US with the rank of captain.

Davis was assigned to the traditionally Black Tuskegee Institute (now Tuskegee University) as the professor of military science and tactics. Other assignments followed, including a stint with the 369th Regiment, New York National Guard.

On October 25, 1940, Davis was promoted to brigadier general, becoming the first Black general officer in the United States Army. The appointment was politically tricky for the Roosevelt administration, because for political reasons the government had announced earlier that same month that the military was to remain segregated, and President Roosevelt was up for re-election in November.

As the US Army Center of Military History noted, Davis's appointment received widespread attention in the national press, for this was the first time that a Black soldier had achieved general officer's rank in the United States Army. In promoting General Davis, *Time* magazine pointed out the administration was violating its announced policy of continued segregation, since he would leave his all-Black command, the 369th New York National Guard Regiment, for the new 4th Cavalry Brigade, containing the 9th and 10th Cavalry Regiments, both of which, as Regular Army outfits, had all white officers. The easiest way out, the magazine advised, would be to retire General Davis on his sixty-fourth birthday due the next July, for "By then the election will be over."

Davis was not retired.

Davis became commanding general of the 4th Cavalry Brigade, 2nd Cavalry Division at Fort Riley, Kansas, in January 1941. About six months later, he was assigned to Washington, D.C. as an assistant in the Office of the Inspector General. During the war, he conducted inspection tours of Black soldiers in the United States Army. As the war drew to a close, Davis was influential in the proposed policy of integration using replacement units.

On July 20, 1948, after fifty years of military service, Davis retired in a public ceremony with President Harry S. Truman presiding.

Six days later, President Truman issued Executive Order 9981, which ended segregation and abolished racial discrimination in the United States armed forces.

Benjamin O. Davis, Sr. died in 1970, but his legacy lived on through his son, Benjamin O. Davis, Jr.

Born in 1912, while his father was serving in an all-White cavalry unit, Ben Jr. resolved to become a pilot. He entered West Point, where he received the same racist treatment as his immediate Black predecessor, Charles Young. His White classmates shunned him. He never had a roommate, and for four years ate his meals alone. His classmates hoped the "silent treatment" would drive him out of the Academy.

It only made him more determined.

In 1941, Captain Davis was assigned to the first training class at Tuskegee Army Air Field (hence the name Tuskegee Airmen), and in March 1942 earned his wings as one of five black officers to complete the course. He was the first black officer to solo an Army Air Corps aircraft.

During the war, Davis and the Black airmen he commanded compiled an outstanding record in combat against the fighter planes of the Luftwaffe. He received the Silver Star for a strafing run into Austria and the Distinguished Flying Cross for a bomber-escort mission to Munich on June 9, 1944.

He again saw combat in 1953 when he assumed command of the 51st Fighter-Interceptor Wing and flew an F-86 Sabre in Korea.

He continued to climb the ranks, and 1954 was promoted to brigadier general (his father's rank), then in 1959 to major general, and on April 30, 1965 to lieutenant general.

At the time of his retirement in 1970, he held the rank of lieutenant general, but on December 9, 1998, President Bill Clinton awarded him a fourth star, raising him to the rank of full general, and said, "General Davis is here today as proof that a person can overcome adversity and discrimination, achieve great things, and turn skeptics into believers; and through example and perseverance, one person can bring truly amazing change."

He died on July 4, 2002, at the age of eighty-nine. He was a true American hero, and his story demonstrates the power of generational achievement. He followed the trail blazed by his father, and then took that trail even further and higher up the mountain.

Isn't that the way it's supposed to be?

5

Five Tips to Own the Room

ike many of the brave pioneers profiled in the previous chapter, whether you're in a classroom, legislative body, office, picket line, driving a truck, or in the executive suite, at some point it's likely you will find yourself The Only Black Man in the Room. While every situation is unique, and you will have to find the answers that work for you, here are five tips to remember during challenging times.

1. Let Your Voice Be Heard!

Don't let the slights go. Don't "pick your battles."

That might not be what you expected to hear. Maybe it's a byproduct of the Black Lives Matter movement and the urgency of our times. Maybe I'm growing more radical as I age. But the time has passed for ignoring racism and bigotry. When you face an indignity in the office, address it head on. That might not necessarily mean calling HR; it could be as simple as calling out a colleague for a cruel remark, or pointing out to them why something they have said is racially insensitive.

And don't just speak up when it comes to the day-to-day issues impacting race and diversity. Remember each day that you have been hired because you have something unique to contribute. So, use your voice when you have an idea.

Especially in those early days of a new job, it can be scary to speak up when everything in you is screaming at you to stay quiet and "get along." But the opportunities ultimately go to those who make themselves visible, just as "the squeaky wheel gets the grease."

Be an Advocate for Diversity and Inclusion

It's not enough to succeed; you also need to lift others up. Many organizations today increasingly carve out time and budgets for diversity and inclusion initiatives. Unfortunately, at some companies, Black employees and consultants can fall into the trap of being perceived as "the diversity person."

You don't want your race to define you first and foremost; but at the same time, you bring perspective and insights that others will lack without you in the room. So, get active and bring your voice to the important work done on these committees.

You can help ensure that they aren't just window dressing or an excuse to say the company is doing something. You can use your voice and your experience to push for what would really move the needle for people of color at your company, whether that is rethinking hiring practices that don't account for the diversity of experience out there or whether it is instituting new policies that ensure that people of color even have a shot during the interview process in the face of subconscious bias in the resume sorting system.

Over-Communicate

So many challenges at work stem from communication errors. Don't let that happen; communicate, communicate, communicate—whether it's about the timeline for a project deliverable or your expectations for a salary. Get used to clearly articulating your thoughts and invest as much time as possible in strengthening your writing skills, which will allow you to stand out from the crowd.

Sit in the Front

Studies have shown that students who sit in the front of their classrooms earn higher grades, which stands to reason, because the front of the room is where the action is and where you have every chance to be fully engaged. So, take the same approach to the world of work, where those who sit in front at conferences conversely tend to be the higher earners. Make yourself visible in every room and don't be shy about assuming your seat at the table.

2. Be a Top Producer

You may learn quickly that you don't have the same benefit of the doubt that many of your peers get. Don't leave any room for ambiguity or confusion about how good you are at what you do. I made it a practice early in my career to always triple check whatever I was working on, no matter how seemingly insignificant—an email, a memo, a presentation.

Yes, it could slow me down and add time to an already packed day. But being detail-oriented and diligent about the most even seemingly insignificant deliverables sends a clear message that you are someone who takes your work—and yourself—seriously.

Create Your Own Support System

Seek out others who know what you have faced and can give you the benefit of their experience. None of us can succeed on our own. Take the time to find people—maybe senior, maybe not—at your workplace who can shed light on their journey and what you can gain from it.

Build Multiple Sources of Income and Opportunity

This may not apply to everyone, but in today's era of frequent job hopping and the gig economy, view your brand with more diligence than the brand of your employer.

Your career will be your responsibility and nobody else will be waking up each day to maximize your opportunities. It's up to you. You may be well advised to not let all of your eggs lay in one basket. Seek out ways to monetize your other passions and interests. By establishing diversification of how you earn money, you can earn yourself the ability to be more fearless and willing to take chances.

Seek Out Your Sweet Spot and Your Niche

Generalists have their time and place, but the world is increasingly skewed to the power of specialists. Find your tiny corner of your trade or organization that you can master and learn more about than anyone else. By devoting yourself to obsession over what you do in a tailored area, you can ensure that you have an advantage over the competition. They will not have put in anywhere near the same number of hours as you and will lack your expertise.

Don't Be Afraid to Ask for Help

People fall behind when they feel like they can't reach out for assistance and have to do it all on their own. That is especially true when you find yourself in a new, challenging environment without a familiar face. So be easy on yourself and ask for help. Lean on your friends. And don't be afraid to admit when you're struggling.

Advocate for Your Full Worth

Don't be shy when it comes to the numbers. Do your homework, don't be afraid to ask, and negotiate. Many people in our community can grow up expecting the worst and ultimately settle for much less than they're worth when it comes to talk salary. Don't fall into that trap—advocate forcefully but politely for what you are worth. You'll be more respected, and you will be in the driver's seat. No HR department is going to go out of their way to ensure you are meeting your compensation potential; it will be up to you to make your case and to not settle for a dollar less.

3. Help Build Workplace Diversity and Inclusion

This is one we sometimes learn the hard way. Work somewhere that deserves you. Don't settle for organizations that don't value diversity and inclusion. There are lots of great companies in America—and abroad as well, in the age of expanded virtual work—that offer opportunities for a diverse range of the workforce, while giving employees opportunities to show what they are capable of.

There are many great, iconic businesses that truly value the work of investing in their pipeline to move more people of color into positions of senior leadership. Find those opportunities and don't tolerate a toxic work environment.

Embrace Similarities, Not Differences

Find ways to build partnerships and bridges with those around you. My experience has been that the vast majority of people don't actively harbor hate or malice; they are more often uneducated, misinformed, or simply oblivious about the corrosive effects of systemic racism. Bigotry can never be tolerated, but try to find understanding, common ground, and areas of agreement with which to build relationships.

Be an Agent of Change

Don't expect the status quo to endure forever, whether that is in terms of your industry or your office location. The winners in the 21st century are those willing to embrace change and roll with the punches.

Be a Mentor and Lift Up Others

Remember to bring others along on your journey. It's not enough to succeed without lifting up others. You may find the most professionally rewarding aspects of your career to be the opportunities to mentor others and give them insights from your own experiences.

Get Comfortable with Being Uncomfortable

The greatest opportunities in life usually fall outside your comfort zone. Get used to embracing discomfort, whether that is stepping into a job even if you don't have as much experience as the job posting asks for, or speaking at a conference alongside experts you admire, or being willing to speak up on an ethical issue you have observed at work. Make it a habit to discomfort yourself, and you will be off into exciting terrain where few of your colleagues may dare to venture.

4. Protect Your Integrity

No reward is worth losing your soul for. In everything you do, I urge you to act as though you are guaranteed to get caught, even if you don't think anyone will ever know. Real success begins with being able to look yourself in the mirror each morning with pride. Take that higher road, and that means get caught being honest. Get caught putting the work in, and get caught not taking shortcuts.

Embrace What Makes You Unique

Don't fall into the trap of living out the expectations of others for who you are. Embrace what makes you special and find ways to be yourself in even professional settings.

Find Your Balance

Don't burn yourself out. We can be so caught up in the pressure to succeed and make our loved ones proud that we flame out in the process. Seek out the things that help you to maintain your sense of self. Your career is a long marathon; pace yourself accordingly.

Strive for Excellence

There's nothing worth doing if you aren't giving it your all. Don't cut corners—let your work reflect your highest conception of yourself.

Be Accountable

Be accountable to others and to yourself. Ask yourself the tough questions. Are you proud of how you spent the day? Are you making the most of your gifts and of your finite time on this planet?

Ultimately, there is no one higher for you to answer to than yourself.

5. Commit to Lifelong Learning

As human beings, we're uniquely capable of learning new facts and skills right up until the moment we take our last breath. You can—and should—continue to challenge your own biases while being humble and recognizing privilege at all levels (not just through the lens of White and male). Strive to incorporate self-awareness into your professional development in the workplace.

Seek Out and Cultivate Mentors

I told you earlier about some of mine, who were mostly family members. Maybe yours are too. Or they might be professors you meet, or they might even just be figures you read about in books. But look to the example of those who came before you. A surefire path to success is to study those people you want to emulate, and then reverse-engineer their path. Look at what steps they took years in advance to get to where they are today.

You don't need to copy anybody. Your journey won't look exactly the same as anyone else's. But there is so much you can learn from mentors, and you can benefit from the wisdom of their mistakes without having to make those mistakes yourself!
View Every Setback as an Opportunity
Even the tough stuff. In virtually any challenge and any storm, you can find a glimpse of a silver lining if you look long enough.

Find Ways to De-Stress

Burnout is real. Don't be a victim and don't be a hero. Our careers are important, but I expect it's true that few of us fantasize about the office on our deathbeds. Remember what exactly is pushing you so hard to achieve things; for most of us, that comes down to maximizing more time with our families and loved ones. Enjoy them and take the time to pursue the hobbies that make you come alive, whether it's exercise or travel or art.

Work hard, but don't let it grind you down. You are more than your job title and you are more than your LinkedIn profile.

Play the Long Game

Don't fall into the trap of short-term thinking. Far too many CEOs make the mistake of driving decisions based on quarterly earnings reports, rather than looking ahead to the strategy for the long term. Outline goals for yourself not just in the months and weeks ahead, but on a longer time horizon. Visualizing your future and goals will allow you to reverse engineer yourself back to the steps you need to take today.

Don't Limit Your Horizons

I've always admired my brother for his insistence on not letting his experiences with racism or pettiness define him. We all maintain different views on how we identify as Black people, but the important thing is to set that identity for yourself. Be vigilant about identifying those around you trying to place you into a convention or box of their own making.

Don't fall into the trap of thinking that there is only so much room at the top for people of color. That's a trope that gets beat into us from watching too many lame movies over the years featuring token Black characters. There's no need to limit your horizons, and it does you no service. Dare to imagine leadership boards that are majority Black and people of color; that's where our demographics are headed in time. So, let's get down to work of making sure that our workplaces reflect the changing demographics of the nation.

The 100 Black Men of America

Thank you for reading this book.

All of the progress we take for granted today is because of the sacrifices that generations before us made. We stand on their shoulders, and we have our own obligation now to do our part for the next generation.

Scripture tells us, "To whom much is given, much shall be required." (Luke 12:48)

I'm confident you have what it takes to succeed. It will depend on your hard work and initiative. But never lose sight of the fact that none of us make it all on our own. We are part of what MLK called "The Beloved Community." It depends on our ability to see our common humanity and to lift each other up, not tear each other down.

And don't just be in it for yourself. As you climb that ladder, pull up the next generation along with you. There are few experiences in this life that you may find more rewarding than that of serving as a mentor.

Remember the words of Martin Luther King Jr.: "Life's most persistent and urgent question is: What are you doing for others?"

Those of you who take on the duty as a mentor have the opportunity to be a model for them of how to flourish, how to succeed, and how to build a life worthy of your dreams. One of the things that makes this program so unique is that we don't just parachute in and out; we are focused on building long-term, one-on-one relationships from middle school to high school, supported by an entire network of Black men.

Don't be too intimidated if you haven't worked much with kids before or aren't sure that you're equipped for the role. Your experience and wisdom will help guide you, as well as being part of an established platform or organization like 100 Black Men of America. If you ever worked with a teacher or coach yourself, you know the idea and you know the difference it can make in a young person's life.

JAMAR J. HÉBERT
Founder and CEO, J. Hébert Companies, LLC. – Newberry, FL.
Author of "Dream It. Plan It. Do It." and "The Only Black Man in the Room"
www.jamarhebert.com – website   info@jamarhebert.com – email

NOTES

NOTES

NOTES

NOTES

NOTES

NOTES

NOTES

NOTES

NOTES

NOTES

NOTES

NOTES

NOTES

NOTES

NOTES

NOTES

NOTES

NOTES

NOTES

NOTES

NOTES

NOTES

NOTES

NOTES

NOTES

NOTES

NOTES

NOTES

NOTES

NOTES

NOTES

NOTES

NOTES

NOTES

Acknowledgements

Through prayer and God's guidance, I would like to humbly acknowledge that this book is the result of a team effort! I express sincere gratitude to those individuals who played an intricate role in bringing this project to fruition. Whether it was a simple word of encouragement or a nudge that motivated me to keep going to get it done, you are appreciated.

To my family: My children Jarius, Peyton, Maddox, and Morgan; you are my blessings, – Thank you for your patience with me during the writing of this book! I love you all more than you will ever know.

Finally, I give all thanks and praise to the Most High - God the Father, the Son and the Holy Spirit for all that I am and all that I hope to be.

About the Author

Jamar Hébert has risen from humble roots in Baton Rouge, Louisiana, to corporate America's heights. His success in the corporate world is the precipice upon which he has built a growing legacy of community activism. He currently resides in Newberry, Florida where he serves in various executive roles including Founder and CEO of J. Hébert Companies, L.L.C.

Leadership is an intrinsic characteristic of Hébert's that manifested in the classroom and later in various boardrooms across the country.

In his native Louisiana, he donated his time and efforts as a member of St Francis Xavier Catholic Church and by volunteering with The Boys and Girls Club, Boy Scouts of America, and Capital High Academy. He understands the importance of leading by example and his favorite quote is *"People the world over have always been more impressed by the power of our example than by the example of our power"*.

To further punctuate his commitment to personal, professional, and community enrichment, Jamar established J. Hébert Companies, L.L.C. in 2016. The multi-faceted organization is an investment company with current holding or considerations in the industries of fashion, entertainment, management, consulting, book publishing, insurance, health/fitness, travel, education, technology, and more. J. Hébert Companies will bridge the gap between consumer needs and wants through strategic investments, brand development, and managing business opportunities.

Hébert continues to set high expectations for himself. In 2020, He co-founded and currently serves as its inaugural chapter president of the **100 Black Men of Greater Florida GNV** Gainesville chapter, a mentoring organization dedicated to enhancing the lives of African-Americans in the community. He is a former Board Member of the Boys and Girls Club of Alachua County and PACE Center for Girls – Alachua and is also a past participant in Leadership Gainesville 39, a year-long community leadership program sponsored by the Gainesville Area Chamber of Commerce.

Hébert is a force in his community as a current and former member of several public service organizations including but not limited to: The 100 Black Men of Metro Baton Rouge where he served on The Capital High Academics Committee and Communications Team, and The National Association for Multi-Ethnicity in Communications (NAMIC), where he was a participant in the L. Patrick Mellon Mentorship Program. Fulfilling a lifelong dream, Hébert was inducted into Alpha Phi Alpha Fraternity, Inc., the first intercollegiate Greek-letter fraternity established for African-Americans. He is a man who understands balance and the principle that charity begins at home. The opportunity to impact his children, Jarius, Peyton, Maddox, and Morgan is an incomparable privilege not taken lightly.

Bolstered by his proven record of leadership, service, and devotion to the enrichment of those in his broad sphere of influence, Hébert released **"Dream It. Plan It. Do It."** In January 2018. The book was more than self-help and inspiration but an achievement guide. Following the success of the book, Hébert has enjoyed speaking opportunities to share the tenets of faith and inspiration gained on his journey. Determined to turn a negative into a positive, Hébert is releasing, **"The Only Black Man in the Room"** on Juneteenth 2022 to inspire readers to use his experience and see the world differently.

CPSIA information can be obtained
at www.ICGtesting.com
Printed in the USA
LVHW030529240622
722030LV00004B/582